".....I have myself hired hundreds of young women
at periods when it required full four weeks of their
earnings to purchase ten yards of calico. Now the
same amount of a young lady's time will purchase two
hundred and fifty yards of prints and calico of equal
or better quality."

Shepherd Tom an early Rhode Island cloth manufacturer
1882.

Also by

Barbara Johannah

QUICK QUILTING

Make a Quilt This Weekend

THE QUICK QUILTMAKING HANDBOOK

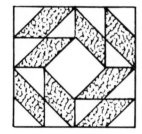

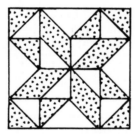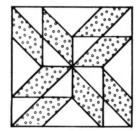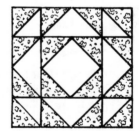

BY
BARBARA JOHANNAH

Shoulder Bag and Super Tote Bag Co-written with Judith Speller
Copyright © 1978, adapted with her permission

How to Make Continuous Bias. Used with permission of the Santa Clara
Valley Quilt Association, P.O. Box 792, Campbell, California 95008

Most of the research for patterns to include in this book was done with the
help and friendship of Judith Speller. It was the most enjoyable time I
spent on the book, Judy.

Thank you Alla, Miriam, J. T. and Vern

Published in 1979 by   Fifth Printing
        Pride of the Forest
        P.O. Box 7266
        Menlo Park, California 94025

Library of Congress in Publication Data
Johannah, Barbara
    The Quick Quiltmaking Handbook
79-88549

ISBN 0-934342-01-6

Credits

  Cover Charlotte Patera

  Photographs

    Wayne Broadbent   J. T. Crossley   Lois Johnson
      Sailboats   Spider Web   String Quilt
      25 Patch Sampler   String Jacket
      Super Tote   Placemats
      Shoulder Bag
      Lone Star

Table of Contents

Section I

Introduction

Planning the Quilt

Getting Started

Section II Quick Quiltmaking Methods, Quilts and Projects

Strips and Strata

Half of a Square Triangle

Quarter of a Square Triangle

Other Projects

Section III

Thoughts on Quick Quilting

Expanding the Possibilities

Have you ever thought about how long it took you to make a quilt and then compared it to how much you used that same quilt? Did you notice that generally the longer it takes you to make a quilt, the less you use it. In addition, if it takes you long enough, you never use the quilt at all, but hang it on the wall or perhaps put it on the bed in the guest room.

Quick Quiltmaking expands the possible uses of quilts. If you can make a quilt in tens of hours instead of hundreds, you may be more inclined to make a quilt for a baby, a small child who plays on his bed, outside on the grass, at the beach, for the dog, etc. In short, quilts to use. That is what quilts are for, to use, to enjoy while using them. The love that goes into the making of a quilt is best enjoyed when it is wrapped around you. We need to touch quilts to enjoy them fully. Watch people at a quilt show. They battle within themselves, trying to honor the requests not to touch the quilts, but often cannot resist. Touch is an integral part of the way we relate to quilts. I think it is important to make quilts that are to be used as well as to be admired, important to the craft as well as to the individual.

Quilts that can be made quickly and can be replaced relatively easy can therefore be used more. Washing in a washing machine becomes practical. In short, faster methods expand the uses to which you are likely to put a quilt, bringing it back to quilts' traditional purpose - to be used.

What Do You Say to People

Who Say It Is Not Traditional?

If someone does not like to use a sewing machine at all, fine; but you should separate personal preference from esthetics and workmanship. If you say that using a sewing machine is not traditional and the results are not handmade, where do you draw the line? Who weaves their own cloth? Who dyes and prints it? Who spins their own thread or makes their own needles?

What is so traditional and handmade about using factory spun, woven and printed fabric? Or factory-made needles, pins, and scissors?

What is traditional and handmade is you individually making the decisions and working with your fabric. If you produced your own fabric, it would most likely be coarse, come in a limited range of solid colors and the crudest of prints. The development and subsequent use of commercially made fabrics has expanded rather than limited our choices giving us an incredible range of type, quality, color, and print to choose from. Your individuality and that handmade quality come through your selection among thousands of possibilities.

The sewing machine is just a tool. A tool with its own unique attributes. A sewing machine does not replace hand sewing. It expands the realm of what is possible. Take advantage of the attributes of a sewing machine rather than having it mimic hand sewing.

The methods in this book take advantage of the size of the fabric you are using and the unique capabilities of sewing machines to make your quiltmaking faster, more efficient, more accurate, and to expand the realm of what is possible.

When to Use Quick Quiltmaking Methods

and

When to Use Templates

Personally, I find it incredible that the sewing machine, in common use for over 125 years, is still not more universally accepted in quiltmaking. How many times have I seen someone admire a quilt top from the front only to disparage it upon turning it over and discovering that it was machine sewn? They admired its workmanship and esthetic qualities, the two most important aspects of a quilt, and put it down arbitrarily because it was done on a sewing machine. I say arbitrarily because being done on a sewing machine has nothing to do with the selection and coordination of colors, prints and fabrics, nothing to do with how well the different design areas of your quilt work together, nothing to do with how well your corners intersect. In short, nothing to do with the quality of the quilt.

What is important is that the finished piece pleases you and that you enjoyed making it.

Below is a comparison of hand sewing and machine sewing with the strong points of each underlined.

Hand Sewing	Machine Sewing
quality of the seam depends upon the skill of the sewer	small, even stitches; strong seams
portable-hand piecing can be taken with you	must work at the sewing machine
maximum versatility	less versatility
slow	fast
relaxing for many sewers	satisfaction with working at the sewing machine depends on the individual

I do not see Quick Quiltmaking methods as a replacement for using templates, but rather as an addition. There are many types of pieced patterns for which templates are the only possibility (that I know of). Also if you are using scraps or are making a single block, the use of a template is appropriate. However, when you are making a pattern that is suitable for my methods and are using yardage, the methods described in this book will give you faster (200% to 800%), more efficient, and more accurate results.

How can this be achieved? 1. By using the size of yardage to advantage to achieve economies of time and efficiency in marking, sewing, and cutting. 2. By taking advantage of the special capabilities of a sewing machine rather than using it to mimic hand sewing.

Recommendations for First Projects

If you are unfamiliar with Quick Quiltmaking methods, I have certain projects I would like to suggest to get you started. The methods described in this book are often easier as well as faster than traditional template-using methods; but like anything else it is only easy after you already know how. Get your feet wet on a small and/or simple project.

To learn the strip method, I suggest you make a Sunshine & Shadow quilt.

To learn the basic tandem method, I suggest you make a few blocks from the Double Four-Patch pattern.

With a comfortable grasp of these two basic Quick Quiltmaking techniques, you can go on to confidently try other patterns.

Choosing Your Fabric

A local quilt store or a mail order quilt business can supply you with a fantastic array of appropriate fabrics, enough for the most self-indulgent of fabriholics and those looking for that special color, print etc. If you need it, quilt shop sales people can help you select your fabric and help you determine the amount of yardage you need.

Fabric Characteristics

Even Weave

The even weave is the most basic of weaves. The threads go under one thread over one thread alternately. The weave is the same in appearance and handling both vertically and horizontally,

Fiber Composition

The first choice today continues to be 100% cotton. In addition to its exceptional qualities of handling, durability, etc., it offers predictability. Cotton is a known quantity. Synthetics in their many varying forms offer a wide range of characteristics, many of which are appropriate to quiltmaking. The trick is to separate the suitable from the unsuitable synthetics. In any case do not use rayon. Its handling qualities are very poor. It has a great deal of diagonal stretch and unravels readily. Always read the end of the bolt to determine the fiber composition.

Fiber Composition in Relation to Ripping

While it is difficult to predict if a fabric will rip nicely or not, 100% cotton fabric generally rips well. Cotton/polyester fabrics rip with varying degrees of success.

Opaque

You should not be able to see through the fabric. To test the fabric, turn it back on itself. Does it show through? Put a darker piece of fabric under a corner of the one you are testing. Does the darker fabric show through?

Firmness of the Weave

The thread of the fabric must be close enough so that the fabric is not flimsy or sheer. If you will be hand quilting, the weave should not be so firm that it causes difficulty in pulling the needle through. Broadcloth plus a good quality muslin are ideal. Muslin sheets are an appropriate fabric for quilts, economical too, a twin flat having about 4 1/2 yards of fabric. Kettlecloth, while too heavy and stiff for hand quilting is easy to piece due to minimal stretching and is a suitable bedspread quilt fabric.

Small Prints and Solids

Generally you should use small prints and solids, avoiding large prints. The scale of the design should be related to the size of your pieces. Avoid checks, stripes, and any obviously linear designs. Whether printed on or woven in, they are almost always crooked. (This caution does not apply when working with templates, because you can continually realign the template each time you use it.)

good   unsatisfactory

Calicos (small, stylized floral designs) are ideal, but so are geometrics, paisleys, etc., and somewhat larger designs.

Wrinkle Free

This is not much of a consideration any more as most fabrics are wrinkle free at least to some extent. Do try to use wrinkle free fabrics - remember you cannot iron your quilt once it is finished.

Stretching

A firm fabric with minimal stretching is ideal. Fabrics that have a lot of stretch, particularily on the diagonal are difficult to work with. Be sure that all of the fabrics you are using in one quilt have the same amount of stretch. If you are not sure of your ability to select fabrics of uniform firmness, staying within one line of one manufacturer would give you fabric with identical handling qualities.

Before Using Your Fabric

Wash and dry your fabric before beginning to mark it. You want any shrinking, dye running, and sizing removal to take place before you make your quilt.

Quilt Size

There are really no standard quilt sizes. Quilt sizes are determined not only by mattress sizes but by the length of the drop you want and whether or not you want the quilt to tuck underneath the pillow.

Quilt Size, Mattress Size and Drop and Pillow Tuck

Give the amount of the drop you want some serious thought. Often one-half or more of the quilt is in the drop. If a full drop is not important to you, don't have one. You will save about one-third of the cost and work. Use a dust ruffle or a bedspread underneath a quilt with a short drop.

How to Determine the Width of the Quilt:

Two times the drop plus the width of the mattress.

How to Determine the Length of the Quilt:

The drop plus the length of the mattress (plus the pillow tuck if you want one).

Mattress Sizes:

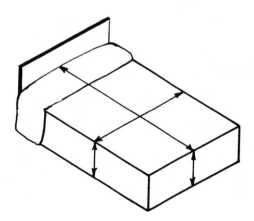

Cot	30" x 75"
Twin	39" x 75"
Extra Long Twin	39" x 80"
Double	54" x 75"
Queen	60" x 80"
King	72" x 84"
Dual Twin	78" x 75"

These are standard sizes. Be safe and measure yours.

Special Purpose Quilts

Baby Quilts

A minimum finished size of 36" x 36".

T.V. Quilts

The quilter's equivalent to an afghan. Approximately 5' by 6'.

Waterbeds

Due to tucking the quilt in the frame, these quilts should have a shorter drop and possibly no border design.

Poster Beds

Quilts for poster beds need to have square corners cut out of them at the bottom of the bed, so that the drop can hang properly around the posts. Keep this in mind when planning your poster bed quilt.

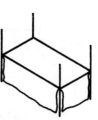

Selection of a Pattern

In selecting a pattern, consider the obvious, such as what your preferences are, who it is for; but also how much time you have available to make the quilt and your level of skill.

Difficulty and Time

One distinction I would like to make is that between level of difficulty and amount of time. We often associate fast with easy and slow with difficult; but that is not always the case. For example, a Lone Star made using the strip method is fast, but diamonds are definitely not easy. The trick is to find a pattern that you like, looks difficult, but is not and is relatively fast.

Level of Difficulty

Shape

Geometric shapes vary as to level of difficulty. Some require more skill to mark, sew and cut than others.

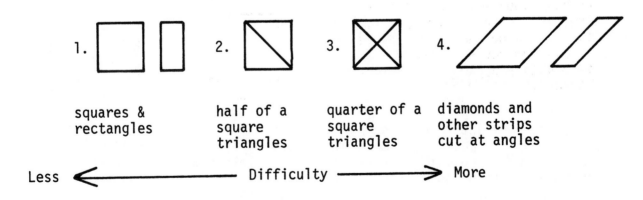

1. squares & rectangles
2. half of a square triangles
3. quarter of a square triangles
4. diamonds and other strips cut at angles

Less ← ————— Difficulty ————→ More

Size of the Pieces

The smaller the size of your pieces the greater the skill you need to do accurate piecing. An 1/8" error can be eased in if the pieces finish 4" or larger. The same 1/8" error cannot successfully be worked into a piece finishing 2". The amount of the error is the same but proportionally it is greater.

Amount of Time

Geometric shapes also vary as to the amount of time needed to mark, sew and cut them, some requiring less than others.

Shape

1. squares and rectangles

2. diamonds and strips cut at angles

3. half of a square triangle and quarter of a square triangles

Less ⟵——————— Time ———————⟶ More

Number of Pieces

Another factor influencing the amount of time is the number of pieces in a project. The more pieces obviously the longer it will take. It would be difficult to set cut-off levels as this varies from person to person so much. I personally consider anything below 300 a small amount and anything over 1,000 to be a lot.

Pieced Pattern Drafting

Quilt patterns follow logical rules of proportion and design. If you understand the internal structure of quilt patterns, you will be able to reproduce the quilts you see in photographs or at quilt shows. You will not be limited to purchased patterns and those copied out of books.

Measurements and detailed instructions are given for many patterns in this book. If you master pattern drafting, you will be able to do additional designs as well as rescale the patterns given in the book, to either a smaller or larger size.

Proportion

If you can superimpose a quilt pattern on a grid or on graph paper, you will have the necessary proportions. The vertical and horizontal lines of the quilt pattern must be on the lines of the grid or graph paper.

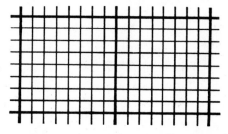

There are many types of graph paper. Four squares to the inch is the most useful for drafting pieced patterns. However, graph paper also comes in twelve to five squares to the inch. A helpful feature of some graph paper is the inch lines are heavier than the rest of the lines.

Quilt patterns fit on grids
with varying numbers of units.

4 Patch   9 Patch   Double Four Patch
16 Patch   25 Patch

Four Patches

If a pattern can be divided in half vertically and horizontally - into four parts - the pattern is a four-patch.

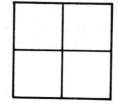 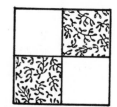

Each of these four squares may be further divided.

They may be divided diagonally.

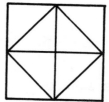 

Double Four Patches or Sixteen Patches

Some or all of the four squares may be subdivided into four squares each.

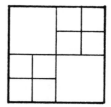 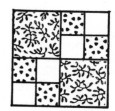

Some or all of these sub-squares may be subdivided diagonally.

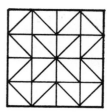 

Barbara Frietchie Star

Nine patches

If a pattern can be divided vertically into three columns and horizontally into three columns, the pattern is a Nine-Patch.

Each of these nine squares may be divided.

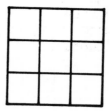 

Some or all of the nine
squares may be divided
diagonally.

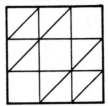 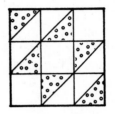

Hour Glass

Some of the nine squares
may be divided into fours.

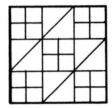 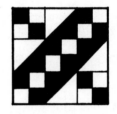

Jacob's Ladder

Some of the small squares
may be divided diagonally.

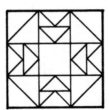 

Double T

Double Nine Patch
Some or all of the nine
squares may be divided
into three columns
vertically, horizontally
or both.

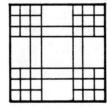 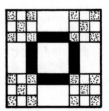

Puss in the Corner

Twenty-Five Patches

Other patterns fit on a grid having five units vertically and five units horizontally. Some of these units are usually divided diagonally or recombined into larger areas.

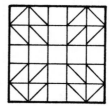 

Jack in the Box

Forty-Nine Patches

A few patterns fit on a grid having seven units vertically and seven units horizontally. Some of these units are usually divided diagonally.

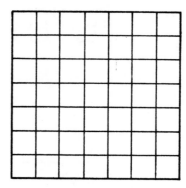 

Peony

Scale

After determining how many units there are along the side of a quilt pattern, you need to decide what scale to use. Each unit can be given as many or as few inches as you wish. If you use whole inches, pattern drafting and marking the fabric will generally be easier.

HOW MANY INCHES YOU MAKE EACH UNIT MULTIPLIED BY THE NUMBER OF UNITS GIVES YOU THE OVERALL SIZE OF THE PATTERN.

Examples

If each unit is equal to 3" and there are two units, then the overall size of the pattern is 6". 3" x 2 units = 6".

Hour Glass

If each unit is equal to 4" and there are three units, then the overall size of the pattern is 12". 4" x 3 units = 12".

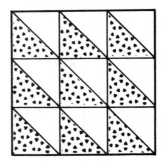

If each unit is equal to 2" and there are four units, then the overall size of the pattern is 8". 2" x 4 units = 8".

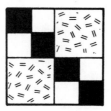

If each unit is equal to 3" and there are five units, then the overall size of the pattern is 15". 3" x 5 units = 15".

Jack in the Box

Remember that these numbers refer to the finished size, rather than the marking and cutting size. Seam allowances must be added.

Changing a Quilt's Size

What if you see a quilt pattern you like, but the directions are not for the size quilt you need? Here are some ways of changing the quilt to the size you want.

Increase or Decrease the Scale of the Pattern

Use the same number of pieces, but make each piece larger or smaller. (Don't increase the scale too much or it will look out of proportion with the rest of the furnishings in the room.)

 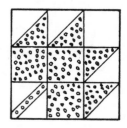

Effect on Difficulty

<u>Increasing</u> the scale makes for easier piecing.
<u>Decreasing</u> the scale makes for more difficult piecing.

Effect on Time

<u>Decrease</u> the scale and the quilt top will take longer to make because you will have more pieces.
<u>Increase</u> the scale and the quilt top will be made more quickly due to having less pieces.

Keep the Scale the Same, but Make More or Less Blocks, Rows, Etc.

If alternating with plain blocks, add or subtract rows two at a time.

 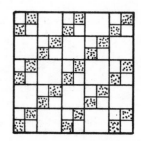

If using lattice strips, add or subtract a row of blocks and a row of lattice strips.

If setting continuously, add or subtract a row of blocks

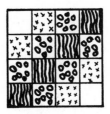 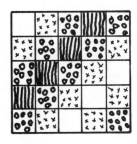

Effect on Difficulty

None

Effect on Time

Increased or decreased in proportion to amount added or decreased.

Add Borders

Make the quilt as directed, but add a border. These can range from fabric strips to intricate pieced borders. A simple fabric strip or several of them is the easiest way to make a quilt larger.

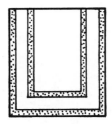 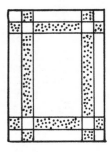

Effect on Difficulty

Also varies with the complexity of the border.

Effect on Time

Varies with the complexity of the border.

How to Figure Yardage

Which method you use depends a great deal on whether you are going out to buy material for a specific quilt or if you are buying ahead for a presently undetermined quilt. This often happens when you have nothing specific in mind, but find a good buy on a particular fabric that you just must have. Of course, if you do not want to do the math, that settles it. Also quilt shops will usually help you figure your yardage. It is one of the services they provide when you buy your fabric from them.

People often ask me how much material it takes to make a quilt without even having a specific quilt in mind! That is like asking how much does a house cost, how tall is a tree or any other general question. Before being able to determine the yardage for a specific quilt, three questions must be answered.

1. What size is the mattress?
2. How big is the drop (and pillow tuck if desired)?
3. What is the scale of the design?

Armed with the answers to these three questions plus some mathematical computations, you can figure out a quilt's yardage requirements.

Method #1 - Precise Method

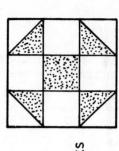

$$\text{Yardage} = \frac{\text{cut size x the total number of this piece in this color in the quilt}}{\text{number of pieces that fit in a yard}}$$

Example: How to Figure the
Yardage for the
white squares in a
quilt composed of
35, 12" Shoo Fly Blocks

4 per block x 35 blocks = 140

1. Determine how many of a particular shape of one fabric are in a whole quilt.

2. Figure in the seam allowance.

$$(1/2" + 4" + 1/2") \times (1/2" + 4" + 1/2") = 5" \times 5"$$

3. Count or determine mathematically how many will fit in a yard.

$$\frac{36" \text{ length}}{5"} \times \frac{44" \text{ width}}{5"} = 7 \times 8 = 56 \text{ maximum per yard}$$

4. Divide into the total pieces in the whole quilt.

$$\frac{\text{Total number of pieces}}{\text{Pieces per yard}} \quad \frac{140}{56} = 2\ 1/2 \text{ yds}$$

Round off considerably higher.
Buy 2 5/8 yards.

5. Repeat with each shape and with each color.

6. Add together. . . . . . .

Congratulations if you made it through with full comprehension. This or some variation of it is the traditional way of figuring yardage. This method is very accurate, slow, tedious and uses a great deal of basic math. There is no guessing with this method. You will know exactly how much you will need. Do allow a little extra though.

Method #2 - Percentage Method

Yardage = finished quilt size plus percentage in seam allowance

Example: Sunshine and Shadow: 6' x 8', 4" squares, 4 colors in equal amounts

1. Determine the finished size of the piece

$$4" \times 4" = 16"$$

2. Figure in the seam allowance.

$$(1/2" + 4" + 1/2") \times (1/2" + 4" + 1/2") = 5" \times 5"$$

3. On a percentage basis, how much larger is the piece with the seam allowance than the finished piece. Divide the answer to Step #1 into the answer to Step #2.

$$\frac{25}{16} = 156\%$$

4. How many yards are in the surface area of the finished quilt?

$$\frac{\text{Width} \times \text{length}}{\text{Number of square feet in a yard}}$$

$$\frac{6' \times 8'}{9} = \frac{48'}{9} = 5\ 1/3 \text{ yds}$$

5. Increase the number of yards in the surface areas of the quilt by the percentage determined in Step #3.

$$5.34 \times 1.56 = 8.33$$

6. Divide proportionally by the number of colors. Round up.

$$\frac{8.33}{4} = 2\ 1/8 \quad \text{Buy } 2\ 1/4 \text{ yds}$$

This is a relatively fast (especially if you round off all numbers) and somewhat less accurate method. It is most appropriate when there are only one or two shapes. There should be a generous amount of extra material figured in to allow for shrinking, areas too small to use on the sides, etc.

Method #3 - Buy Plenty Ahead of Time

A favored method of myself and others is to buy too much in the first place. I purchase at least 3 yards if there will be several colors used, 5 yards if two colors will be needed.

Setting Arrangements for Blocks

The way you put your blocks together (the pattern that they form) is your setting arrangement. Each pattern usually has at least several setting arrangements. Some patterns have setting arrangements which are unique to the pattern while most can be set in one or more of the following arrangements.

Alternate Pieced Blocks with Plain Blocks

Alternating pieced and plain blocks visually separate the pieced blocks from each other. The plain blocks are usually quilted in a design that is different from the pieced blocks, but that enhance the pieced block.

Generally when alternating pieced and plain blocks, there should be an odd number of blocks in both the width and the length so that the quilt appears balanced.

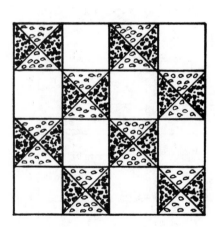

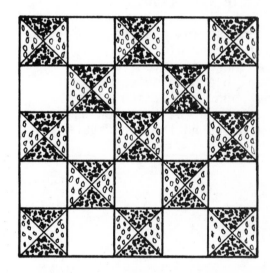

Unbalanced   Balanced

The Number of Pieced Blocks Needed =

$$\frac{\text{number of blocks in width} \times \text{number of blocks in length}}{2} + 1/2$$

As an alternative to the vertical/odd number of blocks setting arrangement above, blocks can be set on the diagonal.

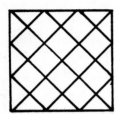

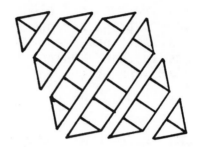

Lattice Strips

Blocks can also be set together with lattice strips. Lattice strips usually visually separate the blocks letting the design in each block stand out. They generally function like a picture frame around a painting. Lattice strips offer a wide range of possible variations.

Lattice strips can repeat a color in the block (in which case there is intentional visual bleeding between the block and the lattice strips and they do not function as frames around the blocks).

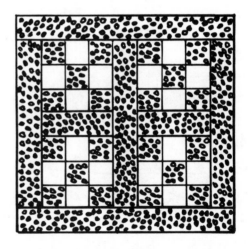

A contrasting color is more commonly used. A contrasting color does function to visually separate the blocks.

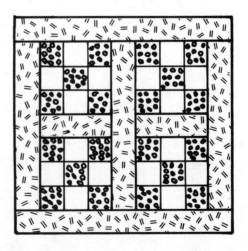

The width of the lattice strips can vary, but should generally
be no more than 1/4 to 1/3 of the width of the block.

Lattice Strip Variations

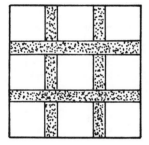 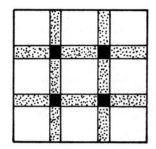

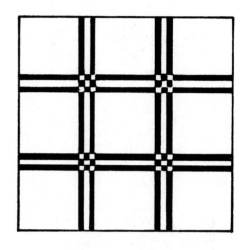

9 Patch Lattice

Setting Blocks Continuously

In setting blocks continuously, you lose the individual
block. The blocks merge together to form an all-over design
that is more complex than the single separate blocks.

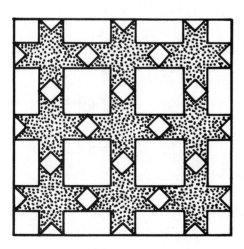 

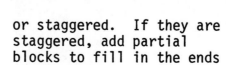

The blocks can be set evenly | or staggered. If they are
staggered, add partial
blocks to fill in the ends
of the rows. | Symetrical patterns
can also be set so
that the blocks
appear to overlap.

If you intend to set the blocks continuously, try your ideas on graph paper first. It is very difficult to visualize what the blocks will look like when set continuously.

Plain Blocks and Continuous Combinations

There are a seemingly unlimited number of combinations when combining plain blocks with continuously set pieced blocks. Here are a few. Again, graph paper is a big help. Draw a few dozen blocks, cut them apart and rearrange.

Setting the Quilt Top - Joining the Pieces

Regardless of the quilting method that will be used, the blocks, lattice strips, if any, and borders, if any, will be joined in some semblance of the following order.

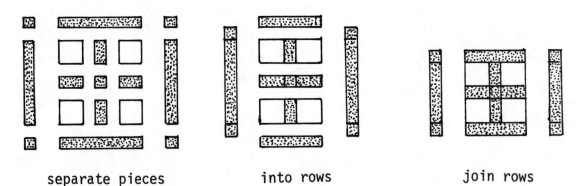

separate pieces   into rows   join rows

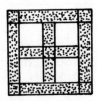

add borders

Borders

Borders Improve and Can Be Added To Most Quilts

    From the narrowest binding strip to the extensive and complex,
borders frame the quilt. If pieced, they add another design
element which adds richness to the quilt. The most crucial aspect
of a pieced border is how successfully it turns the corner. Solid
fabric borders whether of one piece or of strips of fabric offer
a good way of making a quilt larger with little additional effort.

    When adding a solid fabric border, you have several options
as to how the fabric can be cut. If you will be doing decorative
quilting on the border, let the quilting design decide for you.

A quilting design that continues around the corner uninterrupted
is suitable for frame, hoop, and lap quilting (Whole quilt quilting),
but not suitable for quilt as you go.

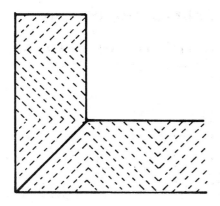

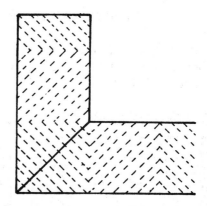

Quilt As You Go
or
Whole Quilt Quilting

Whole Quilt Quilting

Using borders also provides an excellent way of adjusting the size of a quilt. For example, if your blocks are 15" and you want to add only another 6", add a 3" border.

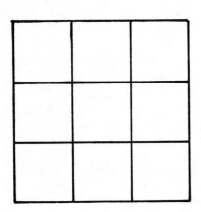
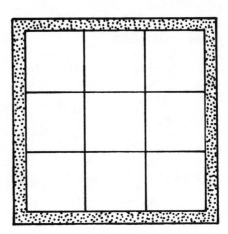

You have the choice of having the border extend all of the way around the quilt

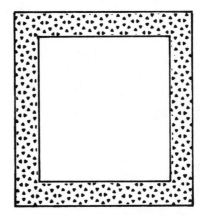

or the border may be just in the drop areas of the quilt. In this case the main design would continue up over the pillows.

Quilt Fillers

The filler is the warmth-providing layer of the quilt. It is sandwiched between the decorative top and the plain backing. There is a wide variety of possible fillers, each having its own advantages and being suitable for different purposes.

Thickness

The various thicknesses of batts available--from 1/4" to 1 1/2"--provide differing amounts of warmth, of course; but there are also other important differences. The thicker the batt, the higher the relief of the quilting. If quilting is close (1" or less), use only a thin 1/4" batt. If the quilting rows are widely spaced (3" or more) a thicker batt will be more difficult to quilt (produce longer stitches), but will produce a higher relief. For machine quilting, a 1/4" batt is easy to work with. Anything thicker may be difficult to work with. Note that thick fillers, closely quilted, reduce the size of the quilt top.

Polyester Batts

Polyester Batts - (not Bonded)

These soft, fluffy batts will remind you of cotton candy when you unroll them. It is difficult to tell where one layer begins and another ends. The batts usually have thick and thin spots which can be evened out by picking off fiber from the thicker areas and putting it on the thinner ones. Since the fibers do separate so readily, these batts must be quilted or tied more closely than the bonded batts. Every 4" is usually adequate. These batts come in a variety of sizes and are cheaper than the bonded batts.

Bonded Batts

Bonded batts are bonded all of the way through. This causes them to be a bit firmer than other batts. They can also have the greatest distances between quilting rows and tying of any type of batt.

Glazed Batts

Glazed batts are polyester batts in which the fibers of the upper and lower surfaces are bonded. The inner fibers remain unbonded. The batts are also soft and fluffy and come in a range of thicknesses. Some brands do, however, have a drawback. When used with polyester or cotton polyester fabric, the batting fibers sometimes come up through the fabric. This gives the quilt the appearance of having a beard.

Comforter Batts

These batts are 3" thick, billowy soft, polyester. A thin non-woven layer of fabric covers them and the two are sewn together about every 6". Tying is most appropriate as quilting stitches would be at least 1/4" long. They are also correspondingly more expensive than thinner batts.

By the Piece Versus by the Yard

Bonded batts can be bought in standard quilt sizes. If you plan to tie the quilt or quilt the quilt as a whole (as opposed to Quilt As You Go quilting), these full-size, bonded batts can save you the time and work of piecing together, which batts bought by the yard require. Avoid the lower quality bagged batts as they are often warped and puckered and, therefore, will be difficult to quilt successfully.

Buying bonded quilt batting by the yard gives you the advantage of being able to buy exactly the amount you want. Moreover, bonded quilt batting rolls out flat. It is ideal for quilting each block individually before joining the blocks. If you wish to use batting bought by the yard for tying or for quilting on a frame or hoop, you will usually need two lengths or two widths of batting.

In this case, butt the two lengths of batting up against each other. (Do not overlap.) Stitch them together by hand, using large stitches. Insert the needle from the underside on each side with each stitch. It is the same kind of motion as tying shoe laces. This stitch holds the two batts together, but also keeps them from overlapping and bunching.

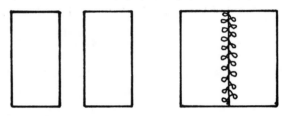

Cotton Batts

Cotton batts are the old standard. They are thin, and, therefore, do not make a puffy quilt. Quilting must be close (every 1") to prevent lumping. Cotton batts come in a variety of sizes and are the least expensive of the various types of batts.

Sheet Blankets and Flannel

If you want a lightweight, thin quilt with a minimum of tying or quilting, a sheet blanket or flannel makes an ideal quilt filler. Since sheet blankets and flannel are woven fabric, you do not have to be concerned with lumping. But, because of the thinness of the fabric, quilting will not show to advantage. Therefore, do not use sheet blankets or flannel if you plan to do extensive or decorative quilting.

Old Blankets, etc.

Old Blankets, Bedspreads, etc.
   Such heavy fillers work best if tied.

Quilting

While the whole process of making a quilt is often called quilting, it is only the in-and-out stitch which holds the top, filler and backing together that actually is quilting.

The quilting can be simple in design and merely functional as in a log cabin. Or it can be elaborate and rival or surpass the beauty of the piecing. This is characteristic of Amish quilts. Quilting is a more subtle form of contrast. The quilting thread color matches or blends with the fabric color.

Quilting achieves its effect from shadow and light and from high and low areas. The quilted areas are pushed down, while the non-quilted areas remain puffed up. When cotton batts were all that were available, the quilting had to be no more than an inch apart to keep the cotton from lumping. With the newer, polyester batts, not only can the quilter get by with less quilting functionally, but more freedom is possible in quilting design.

Design

Quilting, to be effective from a design standpoint, should reinforce the pieced design and, perhaps, provide additional, but not conflicting, design elements.

To get an idea of what you do not want to do, look at commercially made comforters and pre-quilted fabrics. The quilting designs are usually irrelevant to the fabric design.

To emphasize the design of the pieced areas of a quilt, the outline method of quilting is more often used. To do this, quilt 1/8" to 1/4" inside a piece, using the seam as a guide. Be consistent, of course. (If you are outlining a square, you quilt a somewhat smaller square.) The number of pieces in a block that you quilt is up to you. It is traditional to quilt all pieces in a block, but this is necessary only when using cotton batts.

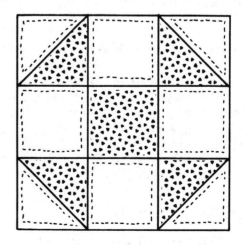

In a two-color block such as the Shoo-Fly, it is more effective to quilt just one color. Here the light color is quilted and the dark color, left unquilted, puffs up.

In a pattern with more than two colors, there are more options as to which colors and shapes to quilt and which not to quilt.

Plain areas of the quilt top present an opportunity for you to do decorative quilting. Plain areas, remember, are whole pieces of fabric rather than the pieced pattern. Examples of plain areas would be lattice strips and plain blocks. Plain areas of printed fabric should have only simple quilting, for elaborate designs will not show to advantage on printed fabric.

A great variety of commercial quilting patterns can be purchased from Quilts and Other Comforts, The Needle Art Guild, quilt shops, and some dime stores if you do not feel up to drawing your own paper patterns.

Transferring the Quilting Design to the Fabric

After you have selected a quilt design, you need a method of transferring it to the fabric. Below are a number of different methods for you to choose from.

1. **Yardstick**   If you want straight quilting lines, use a yardstick and a water-soluable ink pen or a washable pencil.

2. **Stencils**   Use a washable pencil to mark through these reusable patterns. Stencils are one of the most expensive types of pattern, but they are easy to use and reusable.

3. **Paper or Mylar Patterns and Washable Dressmaker's Carbon Paper** Position your paper or mylar template where you want the design to be on your fabric. Pin one side of it. Slide the carbon paper between the pattern and the fabric carbon side down. You may need several sheets. Finish pinning. Trace firmly over the design with a pencil or tracing wheel. When you quilt, if you follow the dots the tracing wheel leaves, you will have perfectly even stitches. You can vary your stitch length with different tracing wheels.

4. **See-Through Method** If your fabric is light in color and your design is done on paper with a black flow pen, place the quilting design underneath your fabric. The design will probably show through and you can trace it onto the fabric with a washable pencil or water soluable pen.

5. **Freehand**   You can, of course, draw freehand and quilt freehand as in outline quilting.

6. **Tailor's Chalk**   Tailor's chalk can be used in much the same way as you would use a regular pencil. However, its line is indistinct and it rubs off too easily.

7. **Water Soluable Ink Pens**   These include many flow pens and "spit" pens. "Spit" pen ink becomes invisable when moistened; but to remove the ink, wash in clear water. Do not use detergent in the first washing as it may set the ink. Also do not iron or heat until rinsing.

8. **Pencils**   Ordinary graphite pencils have long been a standard for marking quilts. Draw lightly for the pencil marks do not always come out easily. Col-erase pencils, erasable drawing pencils, offer a practical alternative. To be safe, choose a pencil which is a lighter or darker shade of the color of the fabric.

Needles and Thread

Use thread specifically made for quilting--a tight twist, cotton thread. Match your thread color to your fabric color. It is traditional for the quilting thread to match the back of the quilt. Also common is to have the thread match the background color of your quilt top. Occasionally each fabric on the quilt is quilted in its matching color. If you wish your hand quilting to be more pronounced and contrast in color with the fabric, use pearl cotton. If machine quilting, use a good quality sewing thread rather than quilting thread. The sewing machine uses two threads making a strong stitch.

Do not be tempted to pick your needle size by how easy the needle is to thread. You want a needle that pulls through the fabric easily. If you have trouble threading the proper size needle, ask someone to thread a whole package of needles for you at once. In five minutes' time you will have enough threaded needles for half a day's quilting. Of course, you can always try an automatic needle threader.

Whether or not to use quilting needles is up to you. Their special size and shape evolved because that is what most quilters wanted in a needle. You may find them too short, etc. Try several different needles and pick the most comfortable. When your piece is finished, no one is going to know what size needle you used.

Basting the Top, the Batting, and the Backing Together
in Preparation for
Quilt As you Go, Machine Quilting or Hoop Quilting

In preparation for machine quilting, quilt as you go or hoop quilting, spread out, wrong side up, the backing fabric. (A muslin sheet is a good choice if you can find the color you want; otherwise, piece the fabric of your choice.) Work out to the edge any puckers or wrinkles in the fabric. Center the batting on top of the backing, and carefully work out any puckers to the edge. Next, center the pieced top, right side up, on top of the batting. Again, work out any puckers to the edge. The secret here is to have three friends help you, one for each corner.

The pieced top, the batting, and the backing must now be temporarily and firmly held together while you are quilting.

Using a contrasting color of thread, baste the three layers together starting in the center and working out to the edges. Continue to baste until the basting threads are no further than 3" apart.

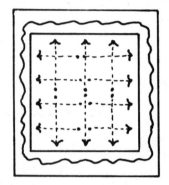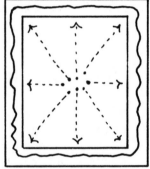

The block, row or quilt is now ready to be quilted.

How to Hand Quilt

Two Methods of Starting and Ending Your Thread

1. Knot
At the end of a single strand of thread, make a small knot with no tail. Pull needle through the piece. Yank thread, popping the knot into the batting. It is easier said than done. Obviously, any knot small enough to go through one side is also small enough to go through the other side. Conversely any knot too large to go through one side is also too large to go through the other side. With a little practice, you will be able to manage it. These knots occasionally pull through with time. A small backstitch will help secure the knot and take some of the strain off of it.

2. **Back Stitching**

Insert the needle an inch or two from where you want to start quilting. Come up where you wish to start quilting. Take a back-stitch. Take a second backstitch splitting the first. Proceed with your quilting. You can also end your thread in the same way. Just reverse the procedure.

Quilting

Using a single strand of thread, make running stitches. This will give you (with practice) an even stitch on the top. In general quilt from the center out. Quilt parallel rows in one direction only. Try to plan your quilting so you can use a full length of thread without knotting off. With complicated designs, you often reach a dead end. If there is another area to quilt close by, first, take a backstitch and, then, slip the needle between the top and the back and come up at the next area to quilt. Take another backstitch and continue quilting. You can travel inside like this for about two inches.

Quilt As You Go

Quilt as you go is not the new method some people think it is. I remember seeing a quilt in the museum in Willits, California that was made in the third quarter of the 19th century that was done quilt as you go. It is the name that is relatively new. Basically, you quilt small sections--either blocks, rows or sections --and then join these already quilted pieces together to form the finished quilt.

This method offers advantages that are hard to beat. A small section of a quilt is easy to carry around with you to work on whenever you have a few minutes. With a small piece, you can hold both the top and back of the piece close to where you are quilting. Quilt as you go quilting uses the same running stitch you already know as opposed to frame quilting which requires learning a new method of stitching.

Securing the beginning and the end of the quilting thread, so it does not show on either the top or the back of the quilt, requires ingenious methods when quilting the whole quilt in one piece. On the other hand, if you start and finish your quilting near the edge of the fabric when doing quilt as you go, you can simply peel back the top to knot the thread.

Joining Quilt As You Go Blocks

1. Sew right sides of the tops of two blocks or rows together by machine.

side view

tops

2. Trim batt to finished size (sewing size) so the batts meet but do not overlap. By hand, sew the batts together as you would lace shoes. Stitch into the batt at least 1/2".

batt

3. Place one piece of backing flat over butted batt edges. Turn under and blind stitch the other.

backing

top

batt

backing

Quilting with a Hoop

If the expansiveness of the quilting design dictates that a quilt be quilted in one piece, then use a quilting hoop. Quilting hoops average 23" across and come in both round and oval shapes. The addition of the stand makes it much easier to quilt. The quilting hoop and stand can be moved around a room and do not take up nearly the space that a quilting frame does.

When quilting the quilt in one piece, work out from the center. Begin by inserting your needle between the top and back, several inches from the point where you wish to start quilting. Bring the needle up at the starting point. Take a backstitch. Take another stitch splitting the previous stitch and proceed with your quilting. To finish off the thread, reverse the process.

Tying

Tying is the quick way of joining the top, filler, and backing together. It is usually thought of as a utilitarian means of holding the layers together, but it can also be decorative. The color of the ties can match or contrast with the colors in the quilt top. Tying can be done with a single or a double strand of yarn. You can tie in the center of the quilt pieces or in the corners. It is easier to tie in the center of pieces, but it can be distracting if the piecing design is complex. Ties in the corners will obscure the precision (or the lack of it) of your work. An acrylic yarn is suggested. Do not use a wool yarn.

Threading the Needle

Here is an easy way to thread yarn through a needle. Cut a narrow strip of paper. Fold the paper over the end of the yarn. Slide paper-covered yarn through the needle eye.

How to Tie

Tying is really quite easy. It is like taking a series of running stitches that are short underneath and long on top. There are three steps-- stitching, clipping and tying.

1. **Stitching**
   Working from the top, take a 1/4" stitch through all layers. Skip to the next place you want to tie. Take another 1/4" stitch. Continue until you are at the end of your yarn. If you have difficulty pulling the needle through, wrap a balloon around the needle. It will prevent you from losing your grip.

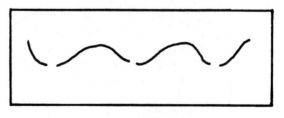

Top View

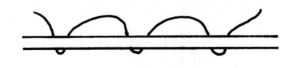

Side View

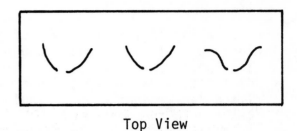

Top View

2. Clipping
Now go back and clip in the middle of each long stitch.

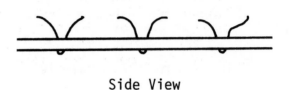

Side View

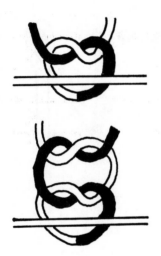

3. Tying
Tie a square knot: right over left...left over right...

and another half knot, right over left, for extra security if you wish.

If You Don't Want Your Ties To Show
Match yarn color to fabric color

Tie in printed fabric rather than solid color fabric

Use a single strand of yarn

Tie from the back. (Finished ties are on the back.)

For Decorative Tying
Contrast yarn color with fabric color

Use a double strand of yarn

Tie from the front. (Finished ties are on the front.)

Tie with two colors threaded on one needle.

Binding

Bindings sewn by hand are more attractive, but are also more time-consuming to do. Let the amount of effort you have put into the rest of the quilt determine whether you blind-stitch or machine-stitch the binding. If you have handquilted, then doing the binding by hand would be in order. Machine-stitched bindings are more appropriate for quilts quickly pieced and tied. If machine stitching the binding, consider using a zig zag stitch. I personally think it is more attractive than a machine straight stitch binding.

There are basically two types of bindings: self bindings and applied bindings. Which type you use depends to a great extent on how you make your quilt.

	Applied Binding	Self Binding
Quilted Whole	X	X
Quilt As You Go	X	
Tied	X	X

Self Bindings

1. **Back to Top**
   This binding style frames the quilt top with a narrow band of the backing color. To make this binding, cut the backing 2 1/2" or more larger than the top. (Trim if necessary after the backing, batt and top have been sandwiched.) Bring the extension around to the top. Tuck under the raw edge and stitch.

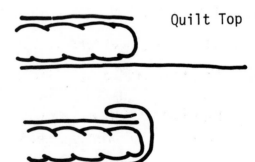

Quilt Top

2. **Top to Back**

    You can also bring the top around to
    the back. In this case, the top must
    be larger than the backing and filler.
    Bring top around to back. Tuck under
    the raw edge, and stitch. This binding
    is appropriate when your quilt has a
    plain fabric border. Make the border
    1 1/2" larger to allow for the binding.
    This binding method is not possible if
    your piecing extends to the edge of the
    quilt top for there will not be enough
    to turn under.

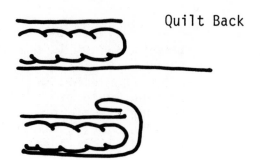

Quilt Back

Finishing Self-Binding Corners

Mitering and squaring off are the two ways in which you can
finish a corner. While mitering is usually associated with hand-
finished bindings, and squared-off corners are more often associated
with machine-stitched bindings, feel free to use either as you please.

Mitering Self-Binding Corners

1. Fold in the seam allowance.

2. Fold again so that the first folded
    edge is precisely on the seam line.

3. Fold in the seam allowance.

4. Fold corner triangle in on dotted line. The fold is a 45° angle.

5. Fold the binding again so that the first folded edge is precisely on the seam line. You may need to refold steps #4 and #5 a few times before you get it right.

Squared-Off Corners on Self-Binding Quilts

Follow Steps #1, #2 and #3 for mitering corners.

Fold the binding again so that the first folded edge is precisely on the seam line.

Applied Bindings

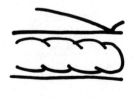

The separate strip method also puts a frame of color around the quilt. More work is involved with this method, because you have to cut the strip and sew an additional seam. It is the method of necessity, however, for many quilts.

Straight Grain Binding

Lynn Maltz, a professional quilt
restorer, who replaces many worn-out
bindings, told me about this double
thickness binding that is suitable
for straight sided quilts. Make 2"
to 3" strips. Fold in half. Iron.
Stitch the cut edge to the top of
the quilt. Bring the folded edge
to the back of the quilt and blind
stitch. I particularily like the
ease of making the strips, the
durability of the double thickness,
and not having to turn under the
edge of the binding on the back
of the quilt.

Lynn also has some good ideas
on how to handle the corners when
using applied bindings particularily
the straight grain variety. Sew
the binding to both the front and
back edges of the quilt. Make sure
the end of the binding strip extends
to the edge of the quilt. Do this
on two opposite sides of the quilt.

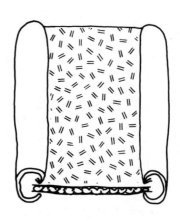

Fold in the edge of another binding
strip. Position it flush with the
edge of the quilt. Pin. Stitch the
binding strip to the quilt top.
As you approach the other end,
cut the binding strip 1/4" - 1/3"
longer than the quilt. Turn the
raw edge in. Finish the seam.
Fold the binding strip to the back
and hand stitch. Repeat for the
other side.

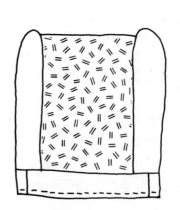

Bias Binding

If your quilt does not have straight sides, you will need to use a bias binding. This binding is a single thickness and is sewn on by hand.

How to Cut Continuous Bias*

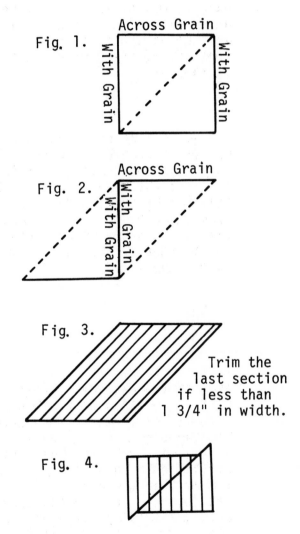

1. Cut a square of cloth in half as shown by the dotted line in Figure 1.

Fig. 1.
Across Grain
With Grain
With Grain

2. Join the two pieces together to form a parallelogram as shown in Figure 2 by placing the two "with grain" sides together. Sew, using 1/4" seam. Press seam.

Fig. 2.
Across Grain
With Grain
With Grain

3. Mark lines 1 3/4" apart as shown in Figure 3. (Lines may need to be up to 2 1/4" apart depending on the width of your seam allowances and the thickness of your batt.)

Fig. 3.
Trim the last section if less than 1 3/4" in width.

4. Seam the parallelogram together to form a tube, moving the first line over one place and matching all other lines, as shown in Figure 4. Cut along continuous line.

Fig. 4.

*As demonstrated by Santa Clara Valley Quilt Association

How to Figure Yardage

1. To find how much fabric to buy for the amount of bias you need, multiply the length (in inches) of the bias you need by the width you plan to cut the bias and find the square root.* This gives the size of the square you will need to buy for the bias.

2. If you already have a square of fabric and you want to know how much bias it will yield, multiply the length by the width of the square and divide by the width of the bias you wish to cut.

*The square root of a number is a number which, when multiplied by itself, equals the original number. (The square root of nine is three; the square root of 36 is six; the square root of 100 is 10; the square root of 625 is 25, etc.)

A 36" square yields about 20 yds of bias.
A 44" square yields about 30 yds of bias.

Top and Back Turned in Binding

On some quilts, such as the Ruffled Baby Quilt, you may not want a narrow band of color around the edge of the quilt. Instead you may want the quilt pattern to end at the edge of the quilt or you may want to insert pre-gathered lace.

1. The edges of the quilted or tied quilt can be turned in and hand stitched.
2. If inserting lace or another trim, sew it facing in, to the right side of the quilt top. Pin the top and backing right sides together and stitch on 3 sides. Turn inside out. Insert batting. Quilt or tie. Blind stitch the fourth side closed. This procedure is most feasible on small quilts.

Some Assumptions

All yardage quantities have been figured with 45" width fabric.

All patterns have been sized for 1/2" seams unless stated otherwise.

Workmanship

Saving time is not the ultimate goal, a beautiful quilt is. Do not be so concerned with saving time that you let the quality of your work suffer. Saving time is not an end in itself. Do not lose sight of quality workmanship.

Extras - Making More than You Need

It is not realistic to think you will get every piece right the first time around. Sometimes you have to rip out your stitches, repin, and resew. Quick Quiltmaking methods being as fast as they are, it is easier to make extra components in the first place than it is to take apart the ones you have already made and resew them. What counts is getting it right the final time and having the first time be the final time as often as possible.

If you find that one of your components is under or oversize, toss it in the string quilt or crazy quilt scrap pile. Use the next component in your quilt top. I make about an extra 5% to allow for any that are not accurate.

Tools and Equipment

Yardstick
Wood or metal
Check wooden yardsticks up against a wall or table for straightness
3" minimum

See-Through Ruler
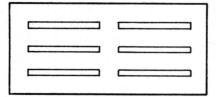
Has spaced slits to mark in. The fastest way yet for marking seam allowances on tandems. Worth every cent of the $2.00 or so that it costs.

Cutting Board
Use one marked with lines rather than dots, 3' x 6'. You may want to cut it in half if you are working on a small surface. The folds in the cutting board cause the inches which straddle the fold to measure 14/16 to 15/16 of an inch. This built-in error in the board does not need to be of any consequence except with triangles which finish smaller than 3". For the greatest accuracy for any project, the best choice is a special plastic coated heavy paper that comes with heavy inch lines and faint eighths. It is not widely available. Try a quilt shop.

For Marking

Water Soluble Pens that do not heat set

Col-erase Pencils
Venus Col-erase is one brand that has worked well for me. They are erasable (on paper) artists' drawing pencils. They come in a wide range of colors and so far have washed out completely.

Graphite Pencils

And of course

Iron
Sharp Scissors
I suggest Gingher's scissors. They are absolutely phenomenal scissors that have to be tried to be believed. They will cut up to 16, yes 16, layers of fabric at once! Available from quilt shops.

Pins
Sewing Machine
Place a piece of tape on the sewing machine a seam allowance width from the needle. The tape should be about 4" long. Generally speaking, no seam lines are marked when doing strip piecing. Rather, you ignore the needle and watch the fabric edge, always keeping it even with the tape. When you sew strips, you get the machine going as fast as it will go. For this reason the short grooves in the machine will not do as a guide.

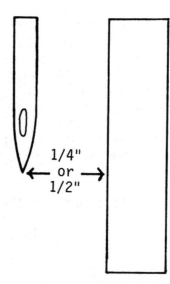

1/4" or 1/2"

Ironing Pointers

Always iron gently. Never stretch the fabric. Let the weight of the iron press the fabric rather than the strength of your arm. Forceful ironing can stretch accurate piecing out of shape. Iron piecing on the right side of the fabric.
When ironing on the front, it is easy to make sure the piece is opened completely. Accurate marking, cutting and sewing are useless unless the piecing is ironed open completely.

correct

incorrect

The Three Musts of Ironing

1.   Iron your fabric before marking it.

2.   Iron seam allowances to one side, generally towards the lighter fabric.

3.   Always iron before crossing a seam with another piece.

Pattern permitting , iron so that one set of seam allowances goes one way and the other set goes the other way. This creates less bulk.

Pattern permitting , iron so that the top seam allowances face the sew- ing machine needle. The sewing machine tends to grab the bottom fabric and push away the top fabric. This works to your advantage when the top seam allowance faces the needle. The ridges caused by ironing the seam allowances to one side lock.

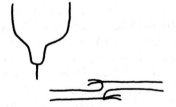

Iron the finished quilt top.

Terms

Strips - The result of ripping, or marking and cutting yardage into long narrow pieces.

Strata - Strips sewn together along their long sides. The fabric from which combinations of squares, rectangles, diamonds or other parrallelograms are cut.

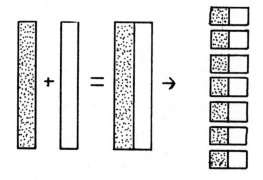

Strips   Strata   Combinations

Half of a Square Triangle   Result of dividing a square diagonally. In tandem piecing, they are made in pairs, sewn together along their long sides.

Quarter of a Square Triangle   Result of dividing a square diagonally in both directions. In tandem piecing, they are made in pairs, sewn together along two of their short sides. Geometrically, Half of Square Triangles and Quarter of a Square Triangles are the same. The difference is which side they are sewn together on.

Tandem Refers to the process and product of sewing a marked piece of fabric and an unmarked piece together and then cutting it apart into combinations. Half of a Square and Quarter of a Square Triangles are two geometric shapes that can be made with this method.

Combinations The pieces resulting when a tandem or strata is cut.

Strips and Strata

Ordinarily you use a cardboard pattern or template to mark individual pieces in preparation for cutting. With Quick Quiltmaking methods, you can do away with the slow process of individually marking and cutting each piece. Instead you can use the yardstick and the cutting board to mark the fabric into approximately 35" long strips. When appropriate, you can also rip the fabric into strips. These long strips are subsequently sewn together and then marked and cut crosswise, resulting in combinations that require only a minimal amount of additional sewing to complete the top.

The first step in working with squares, rectangles, diamonds or any other shape made from strata is to make the strips.

Strata are two or more strips of fabric sewed together along their long sides.

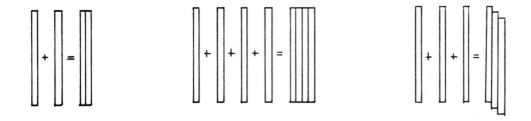

To better help you understand the basics, I will use a 12" Nine-Patch block as an example in explaining strips and strata.

If the Nine-Patch block will be 12" when finished, then each of the pieces will be 4" square when finished. But 1/2" must be added to all sides for the seam allowance. This makes the marking and cutting interval 5".

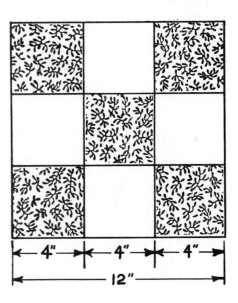

Seam Allowances

I suggest 1/2" seam allowances for three reasons:

1. It keeps your measurements in whole inches.

2. The nature of the sewing method makes 1/2" seam allowances more efficient than 1/4".

3. Your time is more valuable than a bit of extra fabric. When you make a dress that is meant to last a few years, you use 5/8" seams Why would anyone use 1/4" seams on a quilt that is meant to give pleasure for generations?

Ripping Strips

Test Rip

Fast! Fast! If and it is a big if, if the fabric is suitable for ripping. Test rip the fabric first.

1. Clip the fabric for about 1/2" near the selvage and parallel to it.

2. Rip.

3. Examine the ripped edge:

    a. Does it curl? How much?

    b. Is it snagged? How deep?

    c. Is the edge stretched out of shape? How much? How deep?

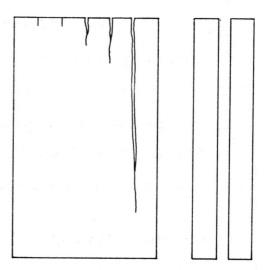

If there is very little distortion of the edge, the fabric is suitable for ripping. The fabric must have no snag or stretching at the seam line. Minor curling can be <u>gently</u> ironed flat. <u>Do not</u> stretch the fabric if you must iron it. If the curling is pronounced, do not even attempt to iron the fabric.

I would suggest that ripping only be used in conjunction with 1/2" seam allowances. Ripping damages the edge of the fabric even on the best ripping fabric. A 1/4" seam allowance just does not allow sufficient leeway.

Ripping the Fabric

If the test rip is successful, proceed using a 4' or less length of fabric.

1. Determine the finished width. In this example it is 4".

2. Add seam allowance.
   Add 1" for 1/2" seams.
   Add 1/2" for 1/4" seams.
   For the Nine-Patch, adding 1/2" to each side equals 5".

3. Starting 1/3" to 1/2" from the selvage, mark the fabric every 5". Be very sure your marks are straight.

4. Cut accurately where you have marked.

5. Rip the fabric into strips.

6. Iron if necessary.

Marking and Cutting Strips

When to mark and cut your strips.

1. You have Gingher scissors or comparable scissors.

2. Your fabric will not rip successfully.

3. You want to adjust the placement of the strips to the print.

4. You will be using 1/4" seam allowances.

How to Mark and Cut Strips

1. Place a square of fabric measuring 35" x 35" or less on the cutting board. Line the straight of the grain of the fabric up with the lines marked on the cutting board.

2. Place the yardstick over the line on the cutting board nearest the left edge of the fabric. Make sure your yardstick extends over the fabric at least an inch at each end. Draw a line on the fabric along the left side of the yardstick.

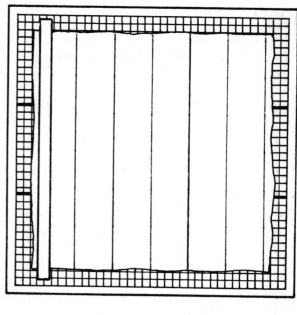

3. Draw lines at 5" intervals. (Remember 4" plus a 1/2" seam allowance on each side equals 5". Thus, if your first line was at the 3" mark on the cutting board, your second will be at the 8" mark--and so on.)

   Note the direction of the marked lines on the fabric to the fold lines of the cutting board.

4. Following the lines you have drawn, cut the fabric into six strips.

   Repeat steps #1 throught #4 with the second fabric-- producing another six strips.

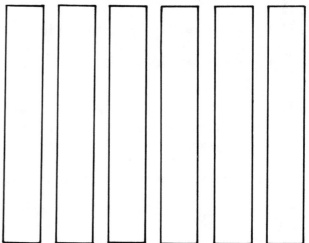

Strata

Sewing the Strips Together

1. Machine stitch the strips in groups of three. Half of your strips are sewn together in this order: a dark strip, a light strip, and a dark strip.

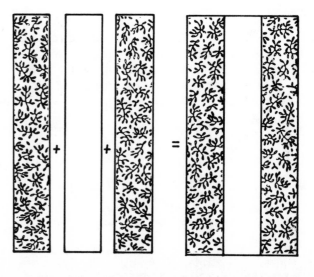

2. The rest of the strips are sewn
   together in a reverse order: a
   light strip, a dark strip, and
   a light strip.

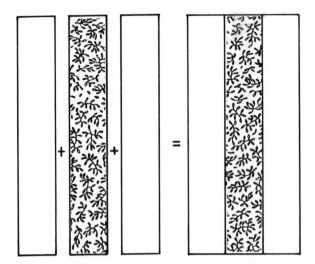

3. Iron all seam allowances to
   one side.

   Place a strata back on the
   cutting board. Line up the
   edges of the fabric with the
   lines on the board. (I am
   starting with a dark-light-
   dark sequence here.)

   Note the direction of the strata
   in relation to the fold lines of
   the cutting board.

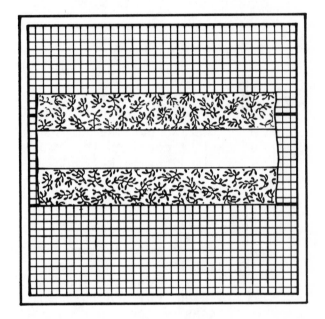

4. Using the yardstick, mark every
   5" (4" plus a 1/2" seam allowance
   for each side).

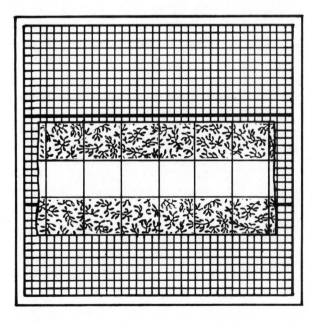

5. Repeat with a light-dark-light sequence of fabric.

6. Cut the strips crosswise on the lines you have just drawn.

7. Sew three combinations together to complete a nine-patch block. Here the two outside strips are dark-light-dark and the middle strip is light-dark-light.

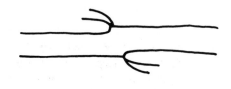

  a. Put two combinations together side by side. The seam allowances of one combination should lie one way and the seam allowances of the other combination the other way. It is easier to match the corners if the seam allowances lie in opposite directions. Read page 51.

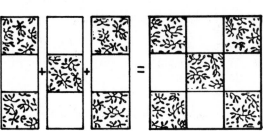

  b. To insure the corners meet accurately, pin the combinations at each intersection. Pin right through the crosswise seam. Using the masking tape guide you have made on your sewing machine, sew the two combinations together 1/2" in from the fabric edge. Following the same procedure, add on the third combination to complete the block.

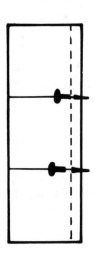

8. Iron all seams to one side

    This is basically how most patterns made from squares, rectangles, diamonds, etc. can be done. Any variations in this method necessitated by other patterns are explained. Once you have started, you will find that the actual process is incredibly fast.

Alternate Methods of Marking and Cutting Your Fabric

1. If you wish to mark the width of your fabric, fold one end of the fabric. Mark as much as you can. Carefully unfold the unmarked end. Extend the lines using the previously marked lines as a guide.

2. If you have Gingher's scissors, try marking one piece of fabric. Layer up to 8 pieces total with the marked piece on top. Layer in pairs right sides together. Carefully cut through all layers while the fabric is still on the board. Now peel off the top two and they are ready to sew. They are already right sides together and the edges are even. No more sorting through all that spaghetti!

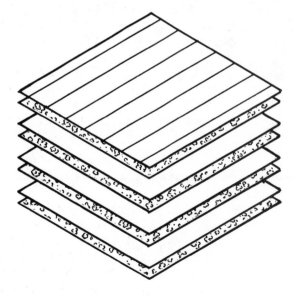

3. If you need very long pieces such as for borders, fold your fabric at the width you need and cut in the fold.

Squares

Including

Trip Around the World, Sunshine and Shadow and Zig Zag

7' x 7'

4" squares

Time - very fast

Difficulty - very easy

Yardage

    2 1/2 yds each of 4 fabrics

    2 1/2 yds each of 4 fabrics

    2 1/2 yds each of 4 fabrics

   2 3/4 yds each of 4 fabrics

Sized for 1/2" seam allowance

Design Possibilities

These are the rainbows of quilts. Rather than contrasting, the colors often gradually flow (blend) into each other.

There are many possibilities:

You can vary one color from light to dark, such as:

You can also follow all or part of the rainbow:

light blue	yellow	↓
medium light blue	yellow orange	↓
medium blue	orange	↓
dark blue	orange red	↓
	red	↓

Or two colors:

light green		light green	
medium green		medium green	
dark green	or	dark green	
light blue		dark blue	
medium blue		medium blue	
dark blue		light blue	

If you wish to design your own all-over squares quilt, consider these variables:

1. The number of squares in your sequence or repeat.

2. The size of your square.

    3" - 4" is suggested for most quilt makers.
    2" for those who want a challenge. Use 1/4" seams.
    5" for those with minimal sewing skills.

The smaller the square and the longer the repeat, the greater the richness and subtlety of the finished quilt.

Making the Quilt Top

1. Refer to the general instructions on working with strips and strata. Make the strips 5" wide (4" finished plus 1" for seams).

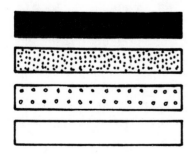

2. Sew the strips together in groups of four along their long sides. Make 1/2" seams.

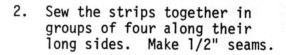
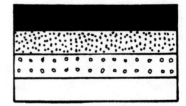

3. Iron seam allowance to one side.

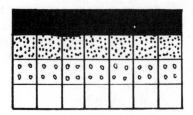

4. Put strata on cutting board, wrong side up. Using your yardstick, mark every 5".

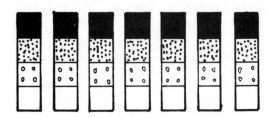

5. Cut on the lines marked.

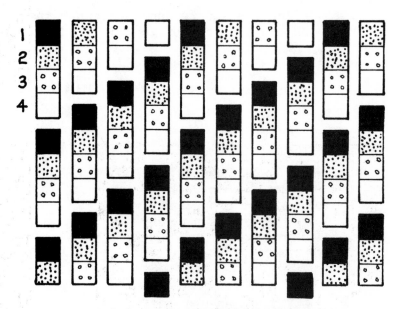

6. The upper left quarter of the quilt.
    Working on a large table or the floor, arrange some of the combinations following the diagram. Sew the combinations together into rows. Some of the rows need only part of a combination at the top and part at the bottom. Rip out the seam separating the combination into the two parts needed. The unneeded portion of a combination of one row is the needed portion of another row. They do not go to waste! For this quarter of the quilt, the first row has two and a half combinations. The second row is pulled up or staggered one square. The third row is staggered two squares. The fourth row is staggered three squares. The fifth row is back in the starting position. The heavy lines show where the quilt is to be divided into quarters.

7. Sew the rows together.

8. Repeat with the other four quarters.

9. Join the four sections to complete the quilt top.

All three of these quilt patterns
can be made from the preceeding
instructions. Try coloring in
the diagrams to see what color
combinations you like.

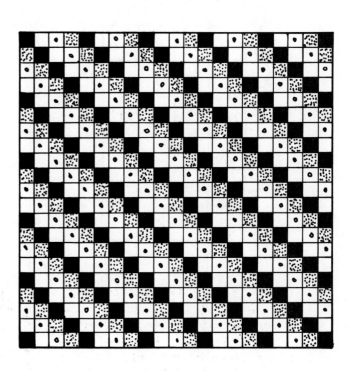

Sunshine and Shadow
Done in rows.

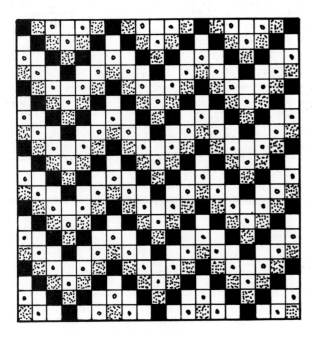

Zig Zag

Done in rows.

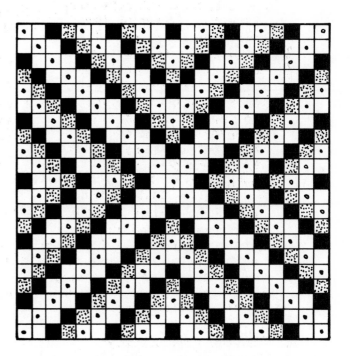

Trip Around the World

Made in quarters.

Ruffles and Eyelet Baby Quilt

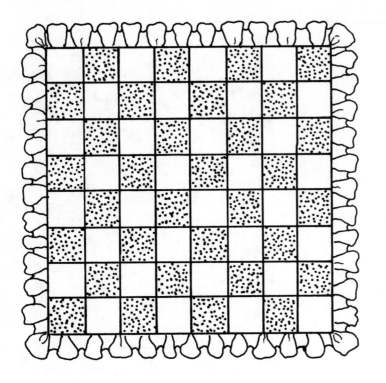

36" x 36"

Difficulty - super simple

Time - very fast

Yardage
  5/8 yd eyelet
  5/8 yd print
  1 yd fabric to line
    the top
  1 yd fabric for back of
    quilt
  4 1/4 yd pre-gathered
    eyelet lace

Sized for 1/2" seam allowance.

This super quick little baby quilt would be ideal if you need a gift for a new-born. The eyelet and lace make this simple checker-board design special.

Making the Quilt

1. Refer to the general instructions for working with strips and strata. Mark both the eyelet and the print fabric into 5" wide strips. (Eyelet will not rip.) Since your fabric is longer than your yardstick, fold one end of the fabric. Mark as much as you can. Carefully unfold the unmarked end. Extend the lines using the previously marked lines as a guide.

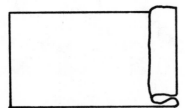
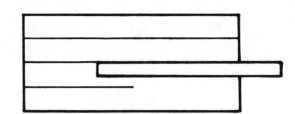

2. Cut out the strips.

3. Sew all eight strips together alternating the eyelet and the print. Iron the strata.

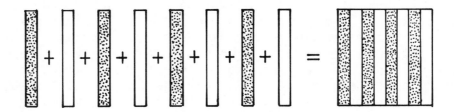

4. Put the strata on the cutting board wrong side up. Mark every 5". Cut on the lines marked.

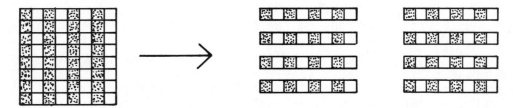

5. Alternate the rows. Sew the rows together to complete the top.

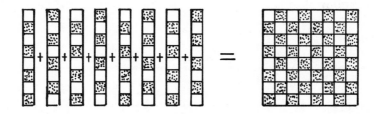

6. Pin pre-gathered lace to the right side of the top; the finished edge facing in. Be sure to allow extra lace at the corners. Finish the raw edges of the lace. Pin the top lining fabric to the wrong side of the quilt top. Sew all the way around. Pin the fabric you have chosen for the back of the quilt to the quilt top right sides together. Sew together, leaving one end open.

7. Turn right side out.

8. Slide batt in.

9. Blindstitch edge.

10. Tie corners of squares.

Diamonds

The blinders of tradition affect us all, I guess. We do most things the way we do because someone else taught us. It speeds up learning to take advantage of the discoveries of others. We would not get very far individually if we had to make every discovery on our own---spinning thread, weaving cloth, piecing, quilts, etc. That ready acceptance and faith in past knowledge can blind us to new discoveries, however, When the situation changes, do we continue to react in the ways that always worked before? Or do we reassess and make some new discoveries? There are so many things we accept without asking why.

When I first devised the Quick Quiltmaking methods for making diamonds, I cut my strips on the bias because I had learned that diamonds must be on the bias. This was a great deal of additional work; it wasted fabric too. Recently I tried making my strips on the grain of the fabric. This produced diamonds which have 2 sides on the straight and 2 sides on the bias. It not only works, but it works better with diamonds made from strips. The anticipated problems did not materialize. I came to the conclusion that at least with diamonds made from strips, there is no reason 2 sides cannot be on the grain.

You probably grasped quite quickly how strata can be made from strips and squares from strata. Diamonds from strata are a bit more difficult.

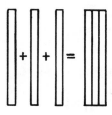

Squares

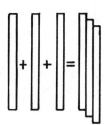

Diamonds

Try thinking of diamonds as skewed or stretched out of shape squares. The strips are staggered when sewn together and the strata cut at a $45°$ angle.

Greater skill is required of the sewer when working with diamonds, so it would be wise, if you are a novice, to try squares first.

The Star of Bethlehem

78" x 99"

Difficulty - most people find
 diamonds fairly difficult

Time - very fast

Yardage
  Diamonds
    Yardage given by position
    of the numbers. You can
    have as few as two different
    fabrics or as many as nine.

Judith Speller

Position	Number of 4 1/4" x 57" Strips Needed
1	1
2	2
3	3
4	4
5	5
6	4
7	3
8	2
9	1

Background Pieces
  4 5/8 yds

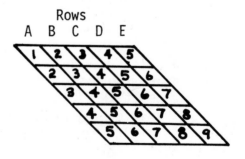

Directions for Diamonds

1. Rip or mark and cut the fabric
    into strips following the general
    instructions. For this pattern
    the strips should be 4 1/4" wide.

2. Sew the strips together using 1/2"
    seam allowance so that the strips
    are staggered. For the Lone Star
    quilt, you will make five different
    sets of strata because there are
    five rows. For Row A sew strip
    numbers 1, 2, 3, 4 and 5 together.
    Stagger the strips 4".

3. Put the strata on the cutting
    board. Near the edge of the
    strata, mark a 45° diagonal
    line. (A 45° line goes through
    the corners of the squares.

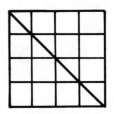

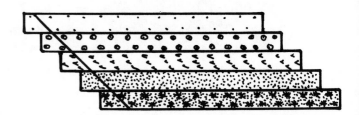

4. Measure the diagonal distance
    of a single strip.

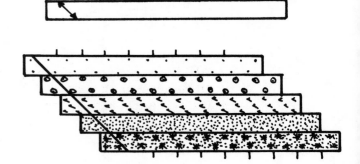

5. Using a ruler, mark off the
    board along the bottom edge of
    the strata at the interval you
    determined. Repeat with the
    top edge. For this pattern
    the interval is 6".

6. Diagonally connect the marks.

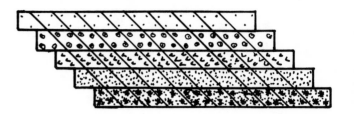

7. Cut the strata into combinations. You must get eight combinations for Lone Star.

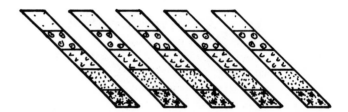

8. Repeat with each of the other sequences of color that you need.

9. Sew the necessary combinations together.

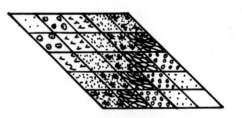

Note: When sewing two rows of diamonds together, the seams of the diamonds must intersect 1/2" in from the fabric edge, rather than at the fabric edges.

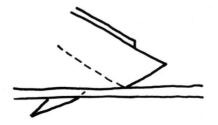

Assembling a Star

When the eight large diamonds are
completed and ready to sew together,
follow this procedure:

1. Sew two diamonds together along one
   side.

2. Start your seam 1/2" from the fabric
   edge and end your seam 1/2" short of
   the fabric edge.

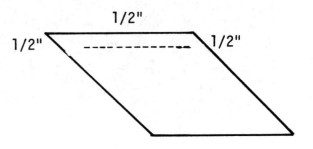

3. Continue to add on the diamond units
   until you complete the circle.

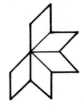

4. On the wrong side, the seam
   allowances in the center of the
   diamonds will fan out in a circle.
   Iron them flat. (If you sew all
   the way to the end of the diamond,
   you will have a layer of 16 seam
   allowances in one place. Sewing
   short of the edge and fanning out
   the seam allowances reduces the
   amount of bulk in one spot.)

5. Do not cut out the background pieces until the star is finished.
   Then measure the sides of the star to get the measurements needed
   for the background pieces. You will need four squares and four
   half of a square triangles. To make the quilt rectangular add
   additional fabric to two opposite sides.

King's X

9 King's X blocks set
continuously. The whole quilt
would be 8 by 10 blocks.
Each block is 19".

76" x 95"

Time - average

Difficulty - King's X - average
           Governor's Palace
           Maze - difficult

The beauty of this quilt would
be enhanced if one of the fabrics
was a stripe. The use of one
striped fabric would have no
effect on the level of difficulty
of the King's X setting arrangement, but would make the Governor's
Palace Maze more difficult due to
the necessity of matching the stripes.

Yardage
  4 5/8 yds dark fabric
  4 5/8 yds light fabric
  You will have enough extra
    combinations to make several
    pillows.

1. Cut each length into 3 equal pieces.

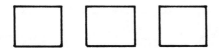

2. After reading the general instructions on strips and strata,
    rip or mark and cut each piece into eleven 4" wide strips.

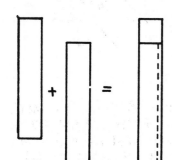

Sew the strips together in pairs
using a 1/4" seam allowance.
Stagger the strips so that one
strip is 3 1/2" longer than the
other.

3. Iron the seam allowances to one side.

4. Premark your cutting board following the diagram below.

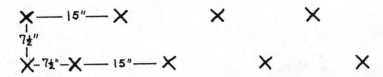

   1st Row - Mark 4 X's 15" apart.

   2nd Row - 1st X - at the left, 7 1/2" below the first row.
             2nd X - 7 1/2" to the right of the 1st X.
             3 additional X's at 15" intervals.

5. Put a strata wrong side up
    within the marks on the
    cutting board. Mark the
    strata into triangles.

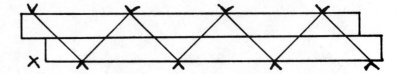

6. Cut on the lines you have marked.

7. Repeat with the other strata.

8. Spread 160 of the triangles out on large tables or on the floor.
    Experiment with them to see what designs you come up with. Sketch
    your ideas on graph paper so you can easily compare them. The trad-
    itional King's X is made in blocks; each block composed of 8 triangles.

Use a 3/8" seam allowance   Use a 1/4" seam allowance to join squares.
to sew the combinations
into squares.

Original designs, such as the Governor's Palace Maze, may be more
suitably assembled in rows. If you do, pick up only one row of
squares. Using your drawing as a guide, sew them together. Return
the completed row to the floor or table. Make certain you have the
row assembled correctly. Pick up the second row and repeat the
procedure. Sew the rows together.

Governor's Palace Maze

Symbolism is possible in piecing as well as in applique and quilting. The Governor was the King's man in Colonial Williamsburg, Therefore, when I designed the Governor's Palace Maze, I used the King's X as a basis. The four squares forming the King's X are in the center pivotal area.

Spider Web

Judith Speller

When Judy first entered a machine pieced and machine quilted
quilt in the County Fair, there was no appropriate category for it.
Consequently it was placed in Miscellaneous. Judy won that year
and each year since. They have been ready for her ever since.
This is her latest winner in the Machine Made Quilt category.
It is made with the strip method and quilted in the ditch.

83 1/2" x 103 1/2"

Time - average

Difficulty - difficult due
  to narrow pieces and many
  intersecting points

Yardage
  8 yds light fabric of spider web
  8 yds dark fabric of spider web
  3 1/4 yds star points
  1 yd fabric for bias binding

Star Points

1. Follow the general instructions
    for making strips. Mark and
    cut or rip 5" wide strips.
    Using template, mark and cut
    out star points. You need 220.

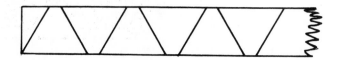

2. Follow the general instructions for marking with strips and strata. Mark and cut or rip 2" wide strips (1" + 1/2" seam allowance on each side) from your two spider web fabrics.

3. Sew the strips together into groups of four strips. Alternate colors. Use 1/2" seams.

4. Using the template as a guide, Mark the fabric into triangles. You need 690.

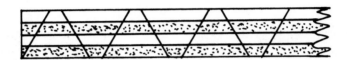

5. Cut out on lines marked.   6. Separate into two stacks.

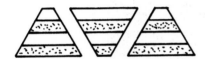

7. Sew six together, three from   8. Sew two star points at opposite
   each stack. Alternate them.   ends onto the spider webs to
                                         complete the blocks.

   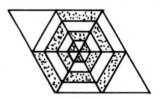

9. Sew the blocks together into rows. Make sure the blocks are always turned in the same direction. There are 13 rows running across the width of the quilt. The ends of the rows will need partial blocks. In the photgraph the rows run vertically.

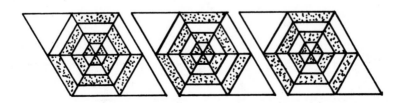

76

Rows 1, 3, 5, 7, 9, 11 and 13

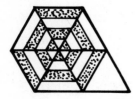

7 complete blocks

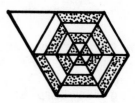

Rows 2, 4, 6, 8, 10, and 12

8 complete blocks

10. Join the rows.

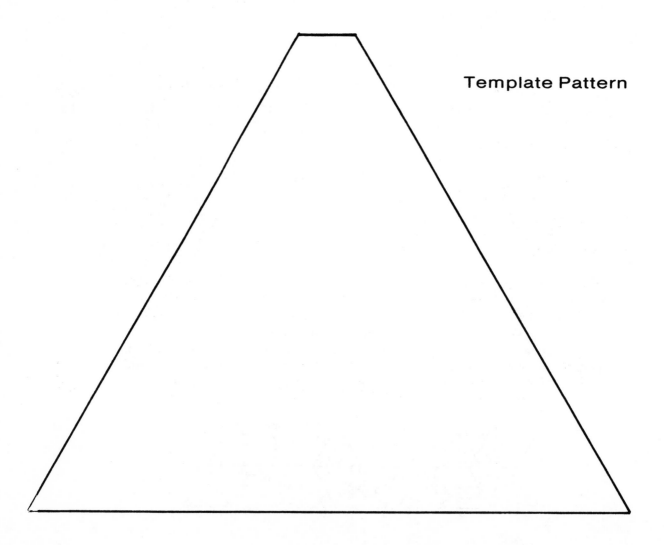

Template Pattern

Half of a Square Triangles

For those unfamiliar with the term, imagine a square divided diagonally in two ◻. The two resulting triangles are half of a square triangles, the most common type of triangle in piecing. They can be put together in a limitless variety of traditional and original patterns. Half of a square triangles usually occur in pairs. When they do, the following method can be used to make them up quickly.

This method of making triangle combinations is probably quite unlike any you have previously used. You will mark one piece of fabric, sew it to the second and finally cut out the pre-made triangle combinations which will look like this ◻.

Read through the instructions and then again while using two practice pieces of fabric before plunging in on the project you have in mind.

Directions for Half of a Square Triangles

Determining the Size of the Triangles

1. Decide on the finished size of the triangle.

2. Add on the seam allowance.

   For 1/2" seam allowance, add 1 3/4". Because of the unique character of these triangles, they must be marked 1 3/4" larger than the finished size - not just 1" as with squares and rectangles.

   Examples:

Finished Size	Marking Interval
3"	4 3/4"
4"	5 3/4"
4 1/4"	6"
6"	7 3/4"

For 1/4" seam allowance, add 7/8".

Examples:

Finished Size	Marking Interval
1"	1 7/8"
1 1/8"	2"
2"	2 7/8"
2 1/8"	3"

(Not easy! For some, including myself, this might be reason enough to use a 1/2" seam allowance.)

In the following example, I will be using a 6" finished size. I will be marking at 7 3/4" intervals. 6" + 1 3/4" = 7 3/4".

Marking Half of the Square Triangles

1. Place a 35" (or less) square of fabric wrong side up on the cutting board. Align the grain of the fabric with the lines on the board as best you can. (Do not be surprised if you cannot as fabric is rarely true in both vertical and horizontal directions.) Mark the board at whatever intervals you have decided on. Pre-mark the board with a different color each time you mark a different size triangle.

   In this example the board is pre-marked at 7 3/4" intervals.

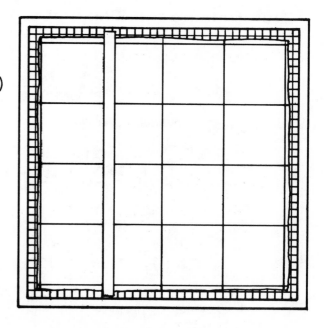

2. Align the yardstick with the vertical line on the cutting board which is nearest the fabric edge. Mark along the yardstick. Continue marking at whatever interval you have decided on, in this case 7 3/4".

3. Mark crosswise as well at 7 3/4" intervals.

4. Get out your see-through ruler. Superimpose one of its center slits diagonally through the corners of a square.

5. IF YOU ARE GOING TO CUT OUT THE TRIANGLES after marking them, mark in the center slit. If using a pencil, make sure it is not too sharp. You do not want a lot of play in the slit. Cut the triangles apart.

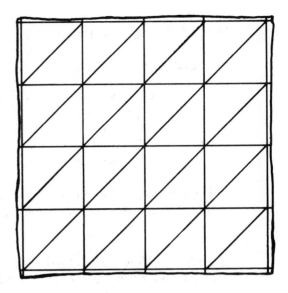

IF YOU ARE GOING TO DO TANDEM PIECING, DON'T CUT OUT THE TRIANGLES. FOLLOW THE INSTRUCTIONS FOR TANDEM PIECING

Tandem Piecing

1. **Marking the Fabric**
   If you want the triangles sewn together in pairs, keep the see-through ruler superimposed diagonally through the square. Instead of marking in the center, mark in the slits on each side of the center slit. (These lines are 1/2" out from the center and will eventually be sewing lines.) Do not draw through the tips of the triangles.

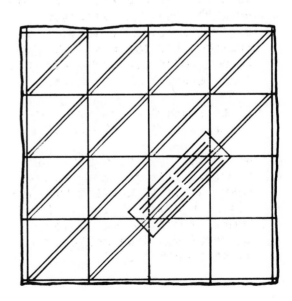

2. **Pinning**

Pin the piece you have just marked to your contrasting fabric, right sides together. This is to hold the fabric together and keep it from shifting while it is being sewn.

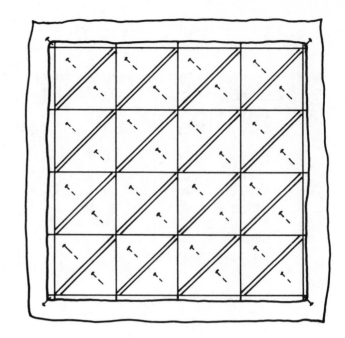

3. **Sewing**

Sew the two pieces of fabric together along the diagonal lines. (Don't sew through the tips of the triangles. Lift your pressor foot up, move your fabric, put your pressor foot down and continue sewing. It is not necessary to cut your threads, but you may wish to hold the fabric flat with your hands to lessen buckling of the fabric.) Remove the pins from the fabric now if you did not do so while you were sewing.

4. **Cutting**

Cut the triangles apart, cutting out the squares first. Cut each square in half between the stitching lines.

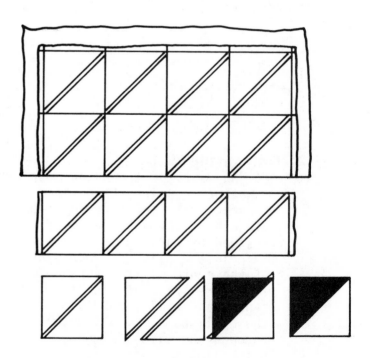

5. **Ironing**

Open triangles and iron seams towards the darker fabric if they would show through your lighter fabric. Trim the triangles. These half of a square triangle combinations should now measure 7". When a 1/2" seam is taken around all four sides, they will finish 6". You now have a stack of pre-made half of a square triangle combinations.

The quantity depends on their size. They are now ready to make up in whatever pattern you have in mind.

Double Four Patch

75" x 96"

17" Blocks

Difficulty - Easy

Time - Average

Sized for 1/2" seam
  allowance.

Yardage
  Blocks
    2 3/4 yds each of two different
    fabrics

  Border
    If you cut the border pieces
    1 1/2" wider, you can turn
    them to the back and use as
    the binding.

    2 5" x 89" (4" x 88" finished)
    2 5" x 76" (4" x 75" finished)

Lattice Strips
  Cut lattice strips after making
  blocks. Measure your blocks.
  If they measure something other
  than 18" including the seam
  allowance, adjust the size of
  your lattice strips to fit.
  9 5" x 18" (4" x 17" finished)
  4 5" x 81" (4" x 80" finished)
  2 5" x 68" (4" x 67" finished)

Making the Block

Double Four Patches are so easy and so incredibly versatile. Each block is made from 16 Half of a Square Triangle combinations. By turning the combinations in different directions, multiple, beautiful patterns are created. Experiment to see if you can design additional blocks. Simply color in half of each square. You could make the quilt all of one pattern or mix patterns. The block used as an example below is the Barbara Fritchie Star. It is in the four corners of the quilt. I understand that the block was designed in her honor. "Shoot if you must this old grey head, but spare my country's flag she said," was reported to be her statement. I could not resist the block or the sentiment.

Make half of a square triangle combinations following the general instructions. Make your lines an even 6" apart.

You need 16
combinations for
each block.

Join combinations
into rows.

Completed
block.

(or use one of the
other patterns)

Double Four Patch Blocks

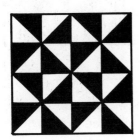

Medallion Baby Quilt

43 1/2" x 43 1/2"

Difficulty - Easy

Time - Fast

Yardage
1 1/2 yd background fabric
(does not include binding
or backing)
1 3/8 yds contrasting fabric

Sized for 1/2" seam allowance.

You Will Need

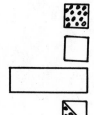

12 contrasting fabric squares 5 1/4"

4 background squares 5 1/4"

4 background rectangles 5 1/4" x 18"

68 background and contrasting fabric half of a square
triangle combinations

Fabric Layout

Background Fabric

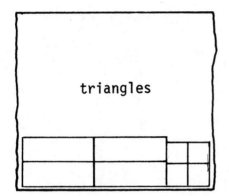

Contrasting Fabric

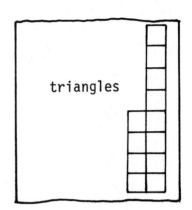

Making the Quilt Top

1. Mark fabric as indicated in the fabric layout diagrams.

2. Cut out the squares and rectangles.

3. Following the general instructions for half of a square triangles, make at least 68 combinations from your contrasting fabric and remaining background fabric. Mark at 6" intervals.

4. Iron seam allowances away from the light fabric or from the fabric you wish to quilt.

5. Top Assembly Diagram

First join the triangle combinations into rows, then join the rows. Iron seam allowances to one side.

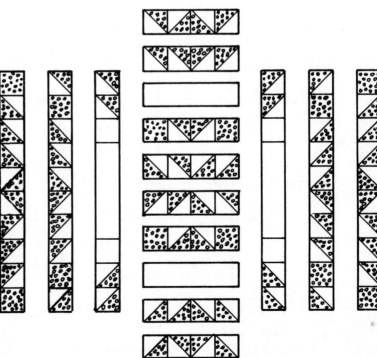

Twenty-Five Patch Sampler

93" x 75"

15" blocks

Time - average

Difficulty - average

Yardage
    3 5/8 yds background
    2 yds medium
    4 1/4 yds dark color

Sized for 1/2" seam allowance.

Kyoko Akao

The entire quilt is made from squares, rectangles and half of a square triangles. None of the blocks are difficult, but you are doing 12 different ones, so take extra care when making the blocks.

Fabric Layout

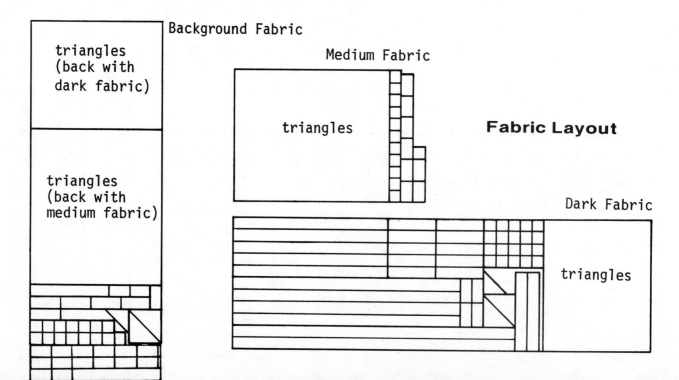

Pieces Needed for the Blocks

	Shape/Size	Color		
		Background	Medium	Dark
1. Triangle Combinations Make half of a square tri- angle combinations following the general instructions. Mark at 4 3/4 intervals.	◁	←191 Combinations→ ←——— 143 Combinations ———→		
2. Square Combinations Make these by following the general instructions for working with strips and strata. The strips should be 4" wide and 26" long. You will need two dark strips and one background fabric strip.	▭	←——— 6 Combinations ———→		
3. Individual Pieces Mark and cut out the in- dividual pieces in the sizes indicated.	4" × 4"	15	12	20
	4" × 7"	16	8	4
	10 3/4" × 10 3/4" triangle	2		2
	7 3/4" × 7 3/4" triangle	1		1
	4" × 10"	5		

Lattice Strips and Border

4. Put aside the fabric reserved for the lattice strips and border until the blocks are completed. Measure the blocks and then adjust the size of the lattice strips and border accordingly if necessary.

Cut from your dark fabric

        2 4" x 88" (3" x 87" finished)
        4 4" x 76" (3" x 75" finished)
        5 4" x 52" (3" x 51" finished)
        8 4" x 16" (3" x 15" finished)

Follow the drawing to make the blocks and pieced border.

Setting the Quilt Top

5. Join the blocks into rows with lattice strips.

6. Join rows and lattice strips.   7. Add outside lattice strips.

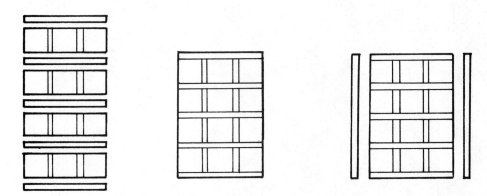

8. Add the pieced border to the top and bottom of the quilt.

9. Sew the side plain border to the side pieced border (which include the pieced corners). Sew the side borders to the quilt.

10. Finally, sew on the top and bottom plain borders.

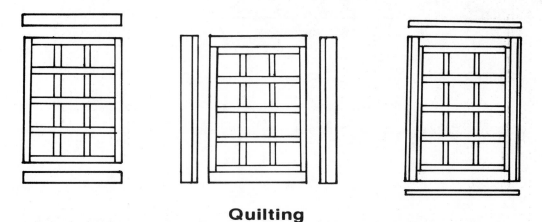

Quilting

This quilt was lap quilted (quilted as a whole piece in Kyoko's lap without a hoop or frame). This should be tried only after experience with other types of quilting, particularily quilt as you go.

You will probably want to quilt on a frame, hoop or quilt as you go. If you wish to quilt as you go, join blocks into rows and quilt each row individually. Quilt the 4 border pieces separately then join the rows and border.

Ocean Wave

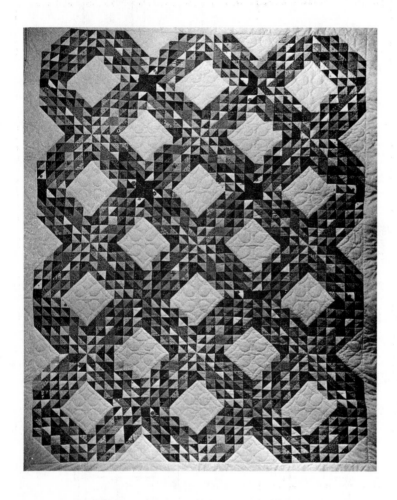

82 1/2" x 108" before quilting

Time - longer than average due
   to the small size of the
   triangles

Difficulty - less difficult
   than it looks

Yardage
   mixed dark prints - 4 1/2 yds
   mixed light prints - 4 1/2 yds
   background fabric border
      and plain blocks - 3 1/2 yds

Gail Dunham

"The real beauty of Ocean Wave is that it looks terribly difficult
and is actually so silly-simple! You can whip one up in no time
and folks will think you've been at it since WW2."-Gail Dunham.

Note: Due to the small scale of the pattern, it is sized for 1/4"
      seams.

Border
1. Cut four 3 1/2" wide strips from your length of background
    fabric. Cut to the proper length after your blocks are made.

Pieces You Will Need for the Blocks

	Piece	Number of Pieces		
		Light Prints	Dark Prints	Background Fabric
2. Triangle Combinations Make half of a square triangle combinations following the general instructions. Mark at 3" intervals. Use 1/4" seam allowance.	◩	←—1152—→ combinations		
3. Single Triangles Mark half of a square triangles following the general instruct-ions. Mark at 3" intervals. Cut out after marking.	◺ ◿	144	144	
4. Cut out a 9" square template from card-board. Place it on the wrong side of the fabric. Mark around it. Cut out at least 1/4" larger.	□			18
5. To make the template for the half of a square triangles, cut the square template in half diagonally.	◿			10
6. Cut the template in half again to make these last four triangles.	△			4

Making the Blocks

The quilt is made from two different rectangular blocks. Each block is made from four sections of triangles surrounding a center square. At first glance the blocks may seem identical; but there is an important difference between the two. The triangles or waves "move" in different directions. A secondary design of pinwheels can be achieved by repeating the same fabric where the "waves" intersect. The Ocean Wave pattern has been divided into rectangular blocks so that you have the option of quilting it by the quilt as you go method.

7. Sew the triangle combinations and single triangles together to make the following four different kinds of triangle sections.

Triangle Section Number 1   24 times

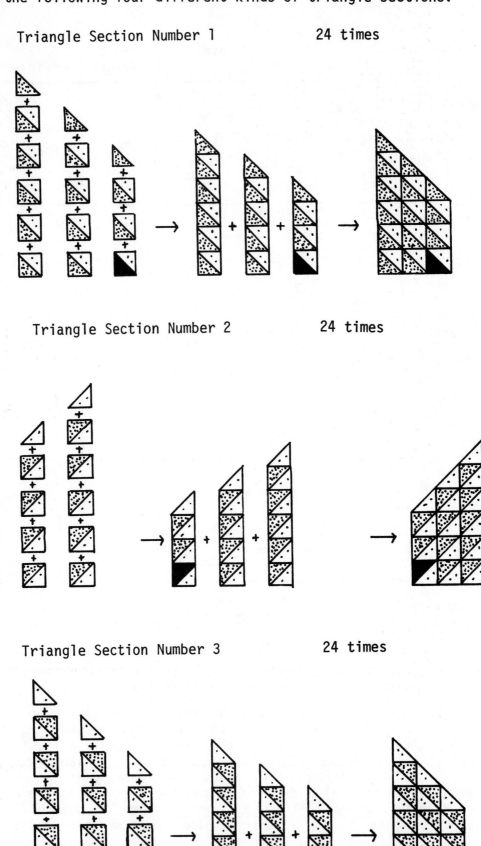

Triangle Section Number 2   24 times

Triangle Section Number 3   24 times

Triangle Section Number 4   24 times

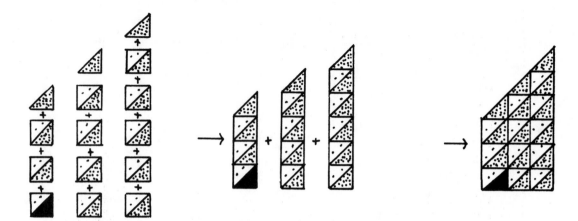

8. Sew the triangle sections and the background pieces together
    to make the blocks and partial blocks.

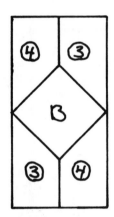

Block A is made from Number 1
and Number 2 triangle sections
around background squares.
Make 12 blocks.

Block B is made from Number 3
and Number 4 triangle sections
around background squares.
Make 6 blocks.

9. There are also partial B blocks. These use the half of a square
    and quarter of a square background pieces rather than squares.
    You will need:

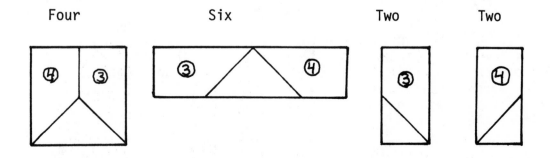

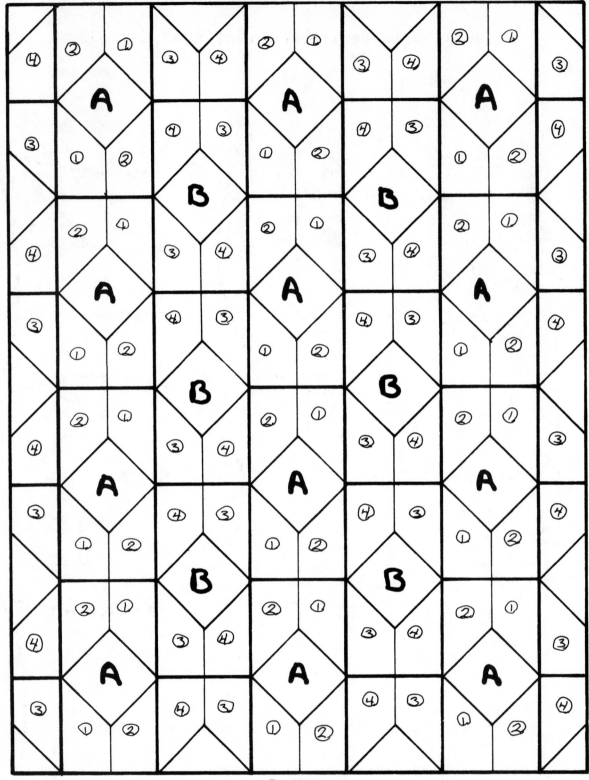

Quilting

10. If quilting as you go, quilt each of the blocks, partial blocks and border pieces separately before joining them. (The partial blocks on the sides and the side border pieces can be sewed together before quilting to reduce the joining work later.) Join the blocks and partial blocks first if quilting the top whole.

Gail's Original Quilting Pattern for Ocean Wave

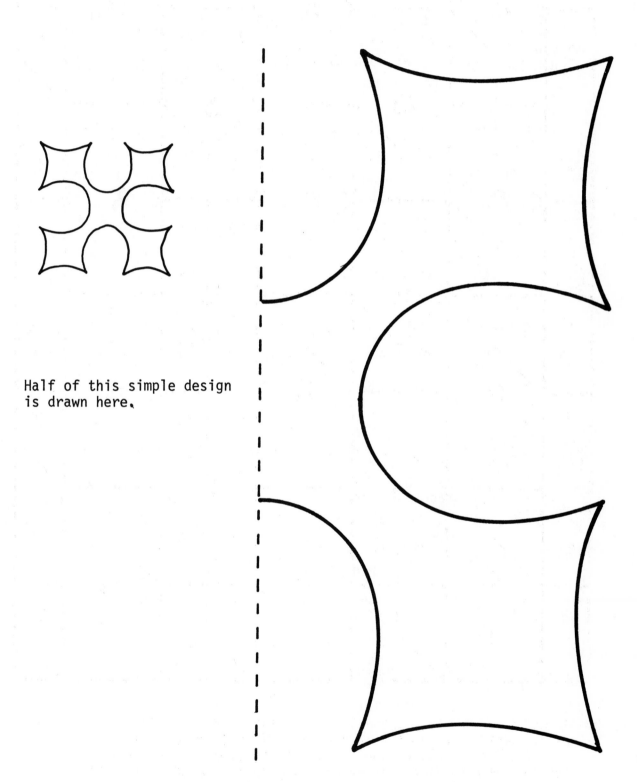

Half of this simple design
is drawn here.

Quarter of a Square Triangles

Quarter of a Square Triangles are very similar to Half of a Square Triangles. With a few variations to your present knowledge, you will soon be making Quarter of a Square Triangles. If you are not familiar with the term, imagine a square divided into quarters The four resulting triangles are Quarter of a Square Triangles. While not as common as Half of a Square Triangles in traditional patchwork, Quarter of a Square Triangles none the less expand your options in Quick Quiltmaking.

Read through the instructions and then again while using two practice pieces of fabric before going ahead with the project you have in mind.

Directions for Quarter of a Square Triangles

Determining the Size of the Triangles

1. Decide on the finished size of the triangle.

2. Add on the seam allowance.

For 1/2" seam allowance, add 2 1/2". Because of the unique character of these triangles, they must be marked 2 1/2" larger than the finished size - not just 1" as with squares and rectangles.

Examples:

Finished Size	Marking Interval
3"	5 1/2"
4"	6 1/2"
4 1/2"	7"
6"	8 1/2"

For 1/4" seam allowance, add 1 1/4".

Examples:

Finished Size	Marking Size
2"	3 1/4"
2 3/4"	4"
4"	5 1/4"
5 3/4"	7"

In the following example, I will be using a 6" finished size. I will be marking at 8 1/2". 6" + 2 1/2" = 8 1/2".

Marking Quarter of a Square Triangles

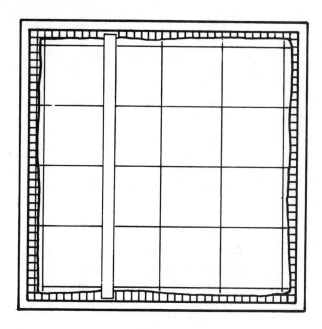

1. Place a 35" (or less) square of lighter fabric wrong side up on the cutting board. Align the grain of the fabric with the lines on the board as best you can. (Do not be surprised if you cannot as fabric is rarely true in both vertical and horizontal direction. Mark the board at whatever intervals you have decided on. Pre-mark the board with a different color each time you mark a different size triangle.

   In this example the board is pre-marked at 8 1/2" intervals.

2. Align the yardstick with the vertical line on the cutting board which is nearest the fabric edge. Mark along the yardstick. Continue marking at whatever interval you have decided on, in this case 8 1/2".

3. Mark crosswise as well at 8 1/2" intervals.

4. Mark diagonally in one direction only, through the corners of the squares.

5. IF YOU ARE GOING TO CUT OUT THE TRIANGLES after marking them, mark diagonally in the opposite direction as well. Cut the triangles apart.

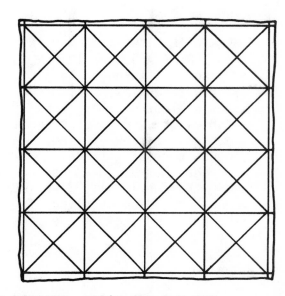

IF YOU ARE GOING TO DO TANDEM PIECING, DON'T CUT OUT THE TRIANGLES. FOLLOW THE INSTRUCTIONS FOR TANDEM PIECING.

Tandem Piecing

1. Marking the Fabric

If you want the triangles sewn together in pairs, get out your see-through ruler. Working in the opposite diagonal direction, superimpose one of its center slits diagonally through the corners of a square. Instead of marking in the center, mark in the slits on each side of the center slit. (These lines are 1/2" out from the center and will eventually be sewing lines.) Do not draw through the tips of the triangles.

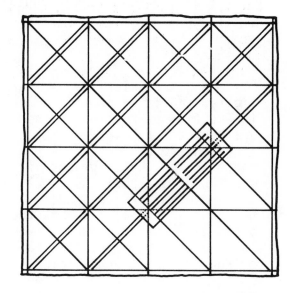

2. Pinning

Pin the piece you have just marked to your contrasting fabric, right sides together. This is to hold the fabric together and keep it from shifting while it is being sewn.

3. Sewing

Sew the two pieces of fabric together along the paired diagonal lines that you just marked in Step #1. DO NOT SEW ON THE FIRST SET OF DIAGONAL LINES THAT YOU MARKED IN STEP #4 OF MARKING QUARTER OF A SQUARE TRIANGLES. (Do not sew through the tips of the triangles. Lift your pressor foot up, move your fabric, put your pressor foot down and continue sewing. It is not necessary to cut your threads, but you may wish to hold the fabric flat with your hands to lessen buckling of the fabric.) Remove the pins from the fabric now if you did not do so while you were sewing.

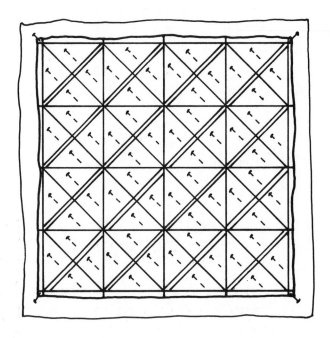

4. Cutting

Cut the triangles apart, cutting out the squares first. Cut each square in half between the stitching lines. Cut also on the remaining marked diagonal lines.

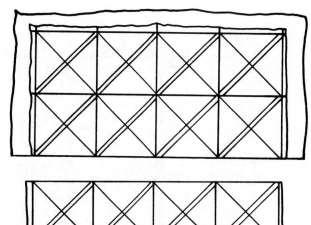

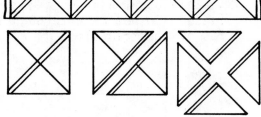

5. Ironing

Open triangles and iron seams towards the darker fabric if they would show through your lighter fabric. Trim the triangles. These quarter of a square triangle combinations should now measure 7 3/4". When a 1/2" seam is taken around all three sides, they will finish 6". You now have a stack of pre-made quarter of a square triangle combinations, the number depending on their size. They are ready to make up in whatever pattern you have in mind.

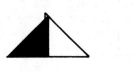

Note that the triangle combinations are of two types.

If you wish to have all of the quarter of a square triangles be identical, follow one of these diagrams for marking and sewing.

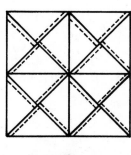 or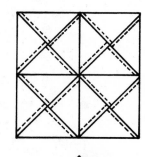

Pinwheel

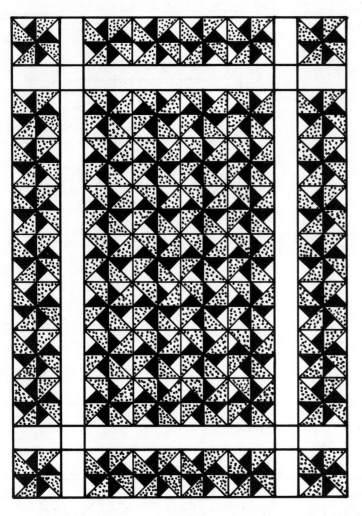

5' 10" x 8' 4"

10" blocks

designed for a
twin bed

Time - slower than
average

Difficulty - average

Yardage for quilt top
Background fabric
4 1/4 yds
Dark Fabric
2 5/8 yds
Medium fabric
4 yds

Sized for 1/2" seam
allowance.

The continuously set blocks cover the top of the bed, while
the border design repeats the pattern in reverse.

Pieces Needed for the Quilt Top

1. Measure and cut out these pieces first
    Background fabric
        You may want to cut them a little longer and trim to size
        after your blocks are finished.
        2   6" x 41"   (5" x 40" finished)
        4   6" x 6"   (5" x 5" finished)
        2   6" x 71"   (5" x 70" finished)
        8   6" x 11"   (5" x 10" finished)

    Medium Fabric
    Following the general instructions for marking half of a
    square triangles, mark the fabric into 6 3/4" squares
    (5" + 1 3/4"). Mark diagonally through the center of each
    square dividing them in half. Cut out the triangles. You
    need 216, 6 3/4" (5" + 1 3/4") half of a square triangles.

2. Background and dark fabrics
   Follow the general instructions for making quarter of a square triangles. Mark at 7 1/2" intervals (5" + 2 1/2"). You need 216 quarter of a square triangle combinations.

Note: Half of the quarter of a square triangle combinations that you make for this quilt are a mirror image of the other half.  One half of the triangle combinations will be used in the main area of the quilt and the reverse half in the border.

Making the Block

3. Sew the quarter of a square triangle combinations and the half of a square triangles together in pairs. Use 1/2" seam allowances. Sew along their long sides to make squares.

4. Join these units together to make 54 blocks, 28 interior blocks and 26 border blocks.

  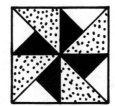   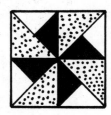

Quilting

5. Decide on your method of finishing the quilt top. If you are going to Quilt As You Go, I suggest you sew the blocks into rows and the border into three pieces first. If not, assemble the entire top before finishing.

Barn Raising

Log Cabin

Yardage
  Center
    #1 3/8 yd
  Light side
    #2 3/8 yd   #7 1 1/8 yd
    #3 5/8 yd #10 1 1/4 yd
    #6 7/8 yd #11 1 1/2 yd
  Dark side
    #4 5/8 yd   #9 1 1/4 yd
    #5 7/8 yd #12 1 1/2 yd
 #8 1 1/8 yd #13 1 3/4 yd

7' x 8' 9"

80 10 1/2" blocks

Time - considering the
 number of pieces, not too bad

Difficulty - moderate, there
 are no intersecting corners
 within the block. The method
 is a bit more involved.

Sized for 1/2" seam allowance.

    Yardage for the top is given by position. Combine pieces into a single color as you wish. This is done to accommodate all of the variations possible with Log Cabin. Use only definitely light fabric for one side and definitely dark fabric for the other. Do not use fabrics that are in between. Your two sides must have strong contrast. Examples would be: light blues on one side and dark blue on the other, solid light pink on one side and green prints on the other or light earth colors on one side and dark earth colors on the other. Try a few ideas with colored pens. When you think you have your color scheme worked out, cut out a few snips of fabric. Pin them together. Are you getting the effect you want? Are you getting enough contrast? Experiment until you do. It really pays off with Log Cabin. Experiment with a few color combinations by coloring in these clusters of blocks.

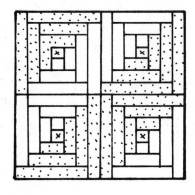
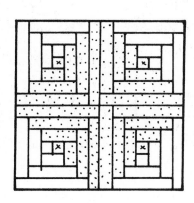
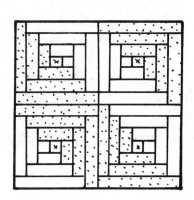

I love the symbolism of this pattern. The rectangles of Log Cabin are the logs of the cabin. The square in the center represents the warmth of the fire in the hearth and is therefore traditionally red. Imagine you are above a log cabin and looking down its chimney.

The number and variety of sizes of the pieces in Log Cabin belie the ease and speed with which it can be made. Quick Quiltmaking transforms Log Cabin from among the slowest of quilts to among the fastest.

The Block

The block is numbered by the order in which it is put together. Starting with the center, #1, the pieces are added one at a time in a spiral. The spiral may be clockwise or counter clockwise but be consistent. One side is shaded in to help you visualize what the block looks like.

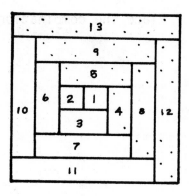

1. Following the general instructions for making strips, use all of the fabric to make strips 2 1/2" wide (for 1/2" seams).

2. Sew strips #1 and #2 together in pairs using 1/2" seams. Do not open.

3. Place several sets of strips on the cutting board. Mark crosswise every 2 1/2". You need a minimum of 80 combinations, but make more.

4. Cut on lines marked. You have marked only one strip, but you are cutting through both.

5. Iron seam allowances away from Strip #1.

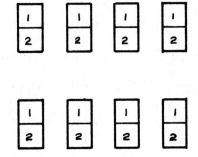

6. Place the combinations from step #5 one at a time on a #3 strip right sides together. Start the first combination about 1/2" down from the end of the strip. Place each succeeding combination aligned flush with the previous combination. The top edge of the second combination should just touch but not overlap the bottom edge of the first combination. Stitch. Pinning is not necessary.

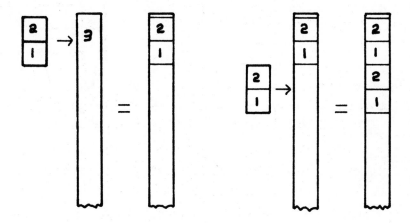

7. Using edges of the combinations as a guide, cut them apart. (You are cutting strip #3 using the combination as a guide.)

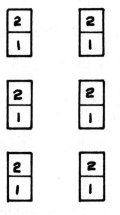

8. Iron the seam allowances away from the center square.

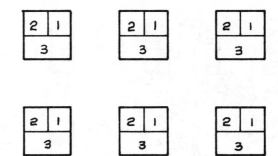

9. Repeat 6, 7 and 8 with each succeeding strip. Make sure your blocks are always growing in the same direction, either clockwise or counter-clockwise is alright. What is important is continuing in the same direction once you have started.

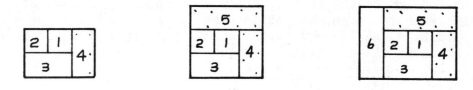

Cross Stitch

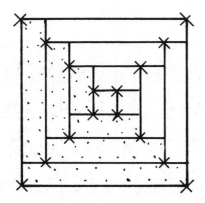

Suggested placement
of cross stitches

There is another alternative for finishing Log Cabins in addition to tying and quilting. It looks like a series of embroidered cross stitches.

Join a row of blocks. Baste together the row of blocks, batting and backing. Using pearl cotton (a crochet and embroidery thread), secure the thread on the back. Make a cross stitch through all three layers finishing on the back. Take a back stitch to lock the cross stitch. Tunnel in the batting to where the next cross stitch is to be made. Come out on the back. (A pin pushed through from the front will accurately locate the spot. Take a back stitch. Make another cross stitch and so on. The back stitches before and after each cross stitch are to secure the cross stitch and lock the tension between the cross stitch and the tunneling, the cross stitch having a firmer tension than the tunneling.

Log Cabin Setting Arrangments

Square Within a Square

In terms of setting arrangements, Log Cabin blocks with two adjacent sides dark and the other two light are subtle, rich, and complex half of a square triangle combinations. Think of them this way when designing possible setting arrangements for your Log Cabin quilt. Mark off a piece of graph paper into squares equaling the number of blocks that you want. Color in half of each square. The setting arrangments given here are traditional ones, but there is no reason not to create your own.

Zig Zag or Streak of Lightning

Log Cabin

String Quilt

Grace Krueger

String quilts allow so much freedom of design that I decided
not to give the specifics of Grace's quilt. Think of it as one of
many possibilities when planning your own string quilt.

Strip Method of Making String Quilts

If you would like the fabrics to repeat in the same sequence in your blocks, follow these directions.

1. Rip or mark and cut strips following the general instructions.

2. Sew the strips together.

3. Measure the width of the strata, 7" for example.   Double the number for the remaining distances.   Mark the board as follows:

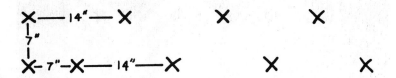

4. Mark the fabric at the intervals you determined.

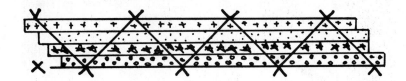

5. Cut the strata into combinations.

6. Cut background triangles of fabric the same size as the combinations.

7. Sew the combinations and background triangles together to complete the blocks.

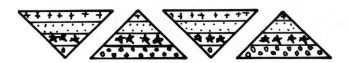 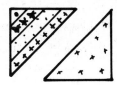

Traditional Method Making this String Quilt

Refer to the instructions for the String Jacket.

Sailboats

Overall quilt 56" x 77"

Design area 36" x 39"

Nine 12" sailboat blocks

Time - fast

Difficulty - easy

Yardage for the blocks
 1 1/2 yds background fabric
 1/2 yd sail fabric
 1/2 yd hull fabric

   Judy took a traditional pattern, Sailboats, and made it special with embroidered anchors and wave and cloud quilting. The quilt was made for her son, Randy, For the borders she used fabric she had on hand.

Judith Speller

Fabric Layout

Background Fabric

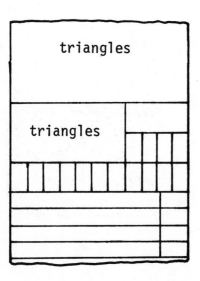

Hull Fabric

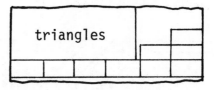

Sail Fabric

Pieces Needed for the Blocks

	Piece	Number of Pieces		
		Background Fabric	Sail Fabric	Hull Fabric
1. Triangle Combinations Make half of a square triangle combinations following the general instructions. Mark at 4 3/4" intervals. Use 1/2" seam allowance.		← 36 → combinations ← 18 → combinations		
2. Using the yardstick and cutting board, mark off your rectangles.	4" × 7" 4" × 7" 4" × 37"	18 4		9

Making the Block

Sew the pieces together in this sequence.

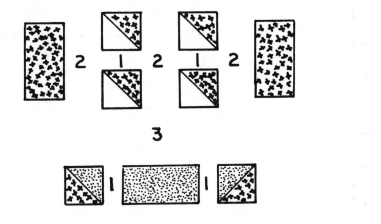

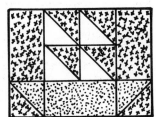

Joining the Blocks

Join the blocks together into three rows.

Join the rows of blocks and the background strips together to complete the main design area.

Border

4. Add border fabric until the quilt is the desired size.

String Jacket

Time - Average

Difficulty - The technique is
 easy; but a piece this size is
 cumbersome to sew with a
 machine.

Yardage
  5 yds total of 5 to 15 different
   fabrics when strips finish 1 1/2
   with 1/4" seam allowance.
  Jacket in photo used 3/8 yds
   each of 13 different fabrics.
  2 yds fabric for lining
  2 yds scrap fabric
  1 yd fabric for binding
  1/4" batting

This jacket uses Dixie Haywood's
idea of incorporating the warmth-
giving filler of the jacket into
the piecing of the jacket, giving
it a quilted look. The entire
jacket is made flat in one piece.
The underarm and side seams are
sewn and bias binding used to
finish the raw edges. If you
want a more fitted jacket, buy
a simply designed commercial
pattern and apply the strings
before sewing the pieces together.

Barbara Johannah

Making the Pattern

1. Have a friend draw around your
   outline on paper. Allow extra
   for looseness and for following
   the curve of the body. If anything, cut it too large. You
   can always trim to fit after
   the strings are on. Cut up
   the center front. Cut a neck
   hole using a commercial pattern
   as a guide if you wish.

Cutting Out the Pieces

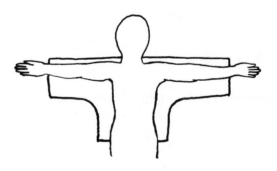

2. Place pattern on fold and cut the lining, scrap fabric and
   batting. They will probably need to be pieced.

Marking the Scrap Fabric

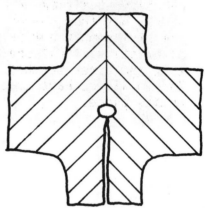

3. Draw a line down the center of the back.

4. Mark parallel rows of lines at a 45° angle across the entire piece. The lines should be spaced at whatever width you want your strips to finish. The lines were spaced 1 1/2" apart for the jacket in the photo. Make sure your lines are going in the same direction as those in the diagram.

Basting

5. Baste the lining, batting and scrap fabrics together every three inches.

Strings

6. Add 1/2" (for 1/4" seam allowances) to the finished width of your strips. For the jacket in the photo, the strips finished 1 1/2" and were cut 2".

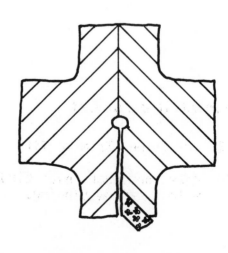

7. Following the general instructions, mark and cut your strips across the width of your fabric. (You need that 44" length.)

8. Starting at the bottom front, put a short piece of one of your strips in each corner right side up and even with the first line.

9. Place a second strip right side down and edges together on top of each of the first strips. Pin and stitch.

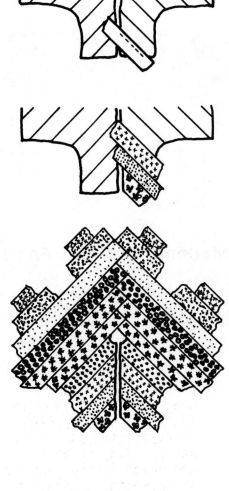

10. Open up the second strips. Continue adding strips until you are ready to pass the back of the neck.

11. Up until this point, it has not mattered whether or not you did one side at a time or alternated sides, but from now on it does. The strips must now be sewn down alternately, first one side and then the other so that they overlap until you have covered the entire piece.

12. Trim the scrap fabric, lining and batting at the back of the neck so it conforms to the strings. Turn the piece over and trim off the ends of the strips that extend beyond the background.

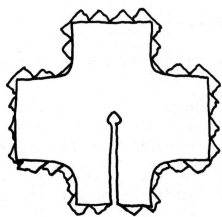

Finish the Jacket

13. Try it on. Trim to fit. Sew up the underarms and sides.

14. Make continuous bias binding. Bind all of the raw edges with a narrow binding.

Super Tote

17" x 17" x 6"

Yardage
  1 yd solid fabric
  (kettle cloth or
  similar recommended)
  2 1/4 yds print
  fabric (of the
  same type as the
  solid)

Sized for 1/2" seam
allowance.

Judith Speller
Barbarajean Santangelo

Fabric Layout

Print Fabric

7" strap
7" strap
7" strap

18" x 18" back lining	18" x 18" front lining
7" x 18" bottom	7" x 18" bottom lining
7" x 18" side	
7" x 18" side	26" x 26" triangles
7" x 18" side lining	
7" x 18" side lining	

This roomy Super Tote can be made
in any one of the patterns in the
Double Four Patch chapter. The straps
go all the way underneath for maximum
strength and durability. Multiple
pockets add to its versatility and
provide space for small things.

Solid Color Fabric

triangles 26" x 26"	full width pocket 13" x 18"

cut pockets as desired

Making the Block

1. Following the general instructions, make 32 Half of a Square Triangle combinations. Mark at 6" intervals. Sew the combinations together to make two blocks from the Double Four Patch chapter.

Assembling the Tote Exterior

2. Sew the blocks to a 7" x 18" bottom piece. Start and stop your seams 1/2" from the edge.

3. Join side pieces following the diagram

Stitch to the edge here.

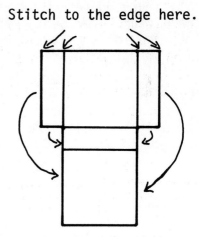

(Seams at the bottom of the lining should begin and end 1/2" from the fabric edge.)

The outside of the Super Tote is now complete.

Straps and lining

4. Join Straps end to end. Fold in 1/2" on each side. Iron.

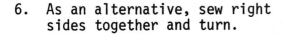

5. Fold in half. Iron. Top stitch 2 or 3 evenly spaced rows. (The first is to close the strap. The second one or two are for strength.)

6. As an alternative, sew right sides together and turn.

7. Overlap the ends of the straps. Stitch securely.

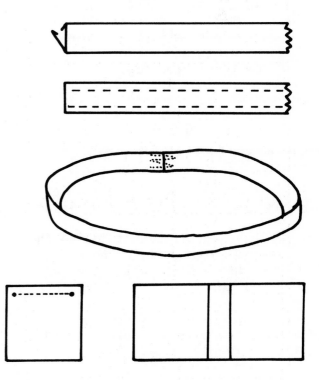

8. Join and 18" x 18" lining square, the 7" x 18" lining bottom and the other 18" x 18" lining square together. Start and stop your seams 1/2" from the edge.

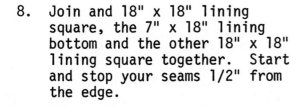

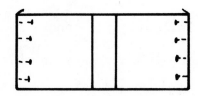

9. Turn top edges in 1/2" and pin.

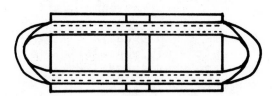

10. Stitch strap to the wrong side of the lining. Stitch several rows for additional strength.

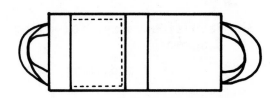

11. Turn under the top edge of the full width pocket twice; turn the bottom under once. Stitch top edge folds. Stitch wrong side of pocket to right side of lining.

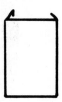

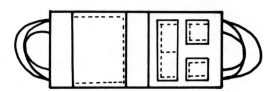

12. Top stitch small pockets as desired to right side of lining.

13. Join the sides of the lining following the diagram. (Seams at the bottom of the lining should begin and end 1/2" from the fabric edge.)

Stitch to the edge here.

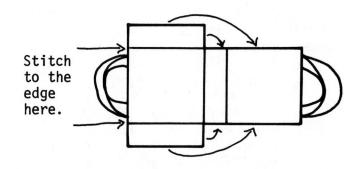

Finishing the Super Tote

14. Turn in top edge of Tote exterior 1/2". Pin. Repeat with lining.

15. Set lining/strap unit inside the pieced outer unit, wrong sides together. Slip stitch the two together.

Your Super Tote is now complete and ready for you to enjoy.

Shoulder Bag

13" x 13"

Yardage
   7/8 yd solid fabric
   2/3 yd print fabric
   two 14 " x 14" squares of
     bonded polyester batting
   two 14" x 14" squares of
     scrap fabric for backing

Judith Speller

The pattern for this shoulder bag is made entirely of triangles. Look at the instructions for the Double Four Patch Quilt. Many other patterns are given which would work equally well.

Fabric Layout

Print

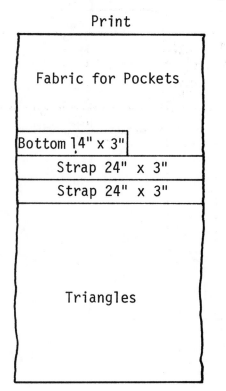

Fabric for Pockets

Bottom 14" x 3"

Strap 24" x 3"

Strap 24" x 3"

Triangles

Solid

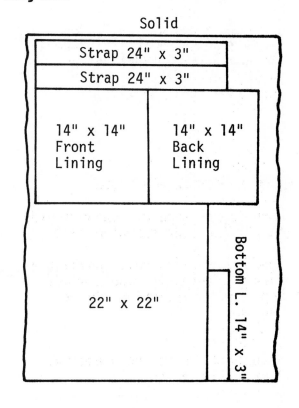

Strap 24" x 3"

Strap 24" x 3"

14" x 14" Front Lining

14" x 14" Back Lining

22" x 22"

Bottom L. 14" x 3"

Making the Triangle Combinations

1. Following the general instructions for half of a square triangles, make 32 triangle combinations. Mark your fabric at 5" intervals.

Making the Blocks

2. Sew the triangle combinations together in one of the patterns in the Double Four Patch instructions. All seams are 1/2".

Quilting the Blocks

3. Baste together a block, a square of batting and a scrap fabric front backing.

4. Quilt the solid color fabric 1/4" in from the seams. (Your knots can be on the backside.)

5. Treating each block as a single layer, join them to the 14" x 3" bottom piece. Start and stop your seams 1/2" from the edge.

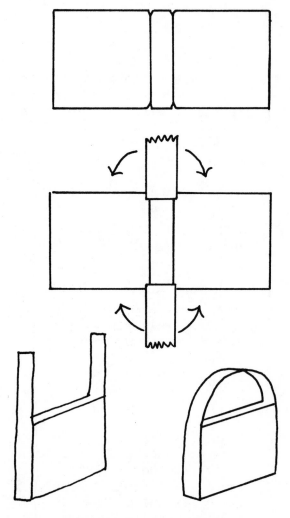

6. Set in strap following diagram, right sides together. Stitch the bottom first. Stop your side seams 1/2" from the top.

7. Join shoulder straps at top.

   The exterior of the Shoulder Bag is now complete.

Lining

8. Topstitch small pockets as desired to right sides of lining.

9. Join the 14" x 14" squares to the 14" x 3" bottom lining piece. Start and stop your seams 1/2" from the edge.

10. Set in straps following diagram.

11. Join shoulder straps at top.

Joining Exterior and Lining

12. Turn in top edges of exterior and lining 1/2". Pin.

13. Turn strap edges in 1/2". Pin. Set the lining inside the exterior with wrong sides together. Slip stitch the exterior to the lining.

14. Using the sewing machine, top stitch the exterior and lining strap together 1/8" from the edge, starting at the very bottom corner at one end and stopping at the opposite corner.

Your Shoulder Bag is now ready to enjoy.

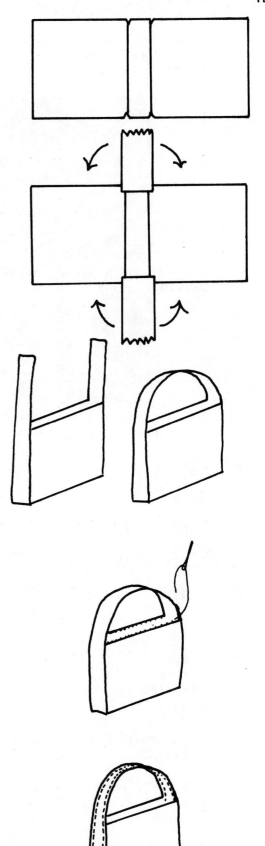

Placemats

Made by Barbara Johannah for Esma Crossley

6 Placemats

10 1/2" x 16 1/2"

Time - Making the blocks
 is fast. Making them into
placemats takes some time.

Difficulty - easy

Diagram of Strip Placement

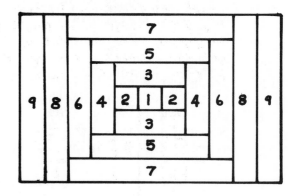

Yardage

Center		Dark sides	
#1	1/8 yd	#2	1/8 yd
Light sides		#4	1/4 yd
#3	1/4 yd	#6	1/4 yd
#5	1/4 yd	#8	3/8 yd
#7	3/8 yd	#9	3/8 yd

These placemats are made from one of the two variations of the log
cabin block. In this variation opposite sides of the block are identical
rather than adjacent sides being the same. Read through the Chapter on
the Log Cabin quilt. The method you will use to make the placemats is
the same, but the order in which you put the pieces together is different.

Making the Blocks

1. Following the general instructions for working with strips, make strips 2 1/2" wide. The strips should be 44" long.

2. Sew these three strips together in this order: #2, #1, #2.

3. Iron seam allowances away from strip #1.

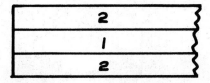

4. Place the strata on the cutting board. Mark crosswise every 2 1/2".

5. Cut on lines marked.

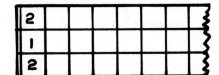

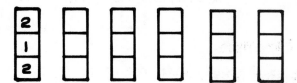

6. Place the combinations one at a time on a #3 strip right sides together. Start the first combination down about 1/2" from the end of the strip. Place each succeeding combination aligned flush with the previous combination. The top edge of the second combination should just touch but not overlap the bottom edge of the first combination. Stitch. Pinning is not necessary.

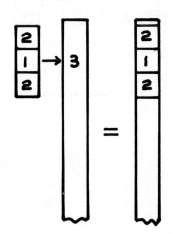

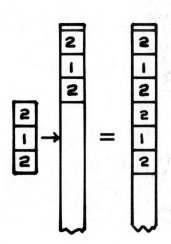

7. Using the edges of the combinations as a guide, cut them apart. (You are cutting strip #3 using the combinations as a guide.)

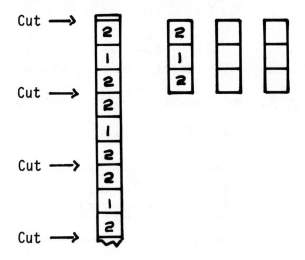

8. Iron the seam allowances away from the center square.

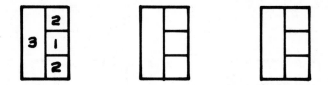

9. Repeat with the other #3 strip on the opposite side of the block.

10. Continue to build the block following the numbered sequence.

Making the Placemats

11. Cut lightweight interfacing 1/4" smaller than the finished size of the placemat. Cut the backing fabric the same size as the blocks.

12. Sew the backing fabric to the quilt block, right sides together. Leave an opening.

13. Turn inside out.

14. Slide in the interfacing.

15. Blind stitch.

16. Hand quilt, machine quilt or cross stitch. The placemats in the photo were machine quilted in matching thread.

Yardage Charts

Maximum Number of Pieces Possible
Not Including the Selvage
Allow Extra for Shrinking, Uneven ends, etc.

Half of a Square Triangles

(Divide by 2 for the Number of Combinations)

Finished Size	Seam Allowance (inches)	Marked Size	Length in Yards (45" Width)	Number of Pieces
1	1/4	1 7/8	1	828
1 1/8	1/4	2	1	748
2	1/4	2 7/8	1	360
2 1/8	1/4	3	1	308
3	1/4	3 7/8	1	198
3 1/8	1/4	4	1	176
3	1/2	4 3/4	1	126
3 1/4	1/2	5	1	112
4	1/2	5 3/4	1	84
4 1/4	1/2	6	7/8	70
5	1/2	6 3/4	1	60
5 1/4	1/2	7	1	60
6	1/2	7 3/4	1	40
6 1/4	1/2	8	1	40
7	1/2	8 3/4	1	40
7 1/4	1/2	9	7/8	24
8	1/2	9 3/4	7/8	24
8 1/4	1/2	10	7/8	24
9	1/2	10 3/4	1	24
9 1/4	1/2	11	1	24
10	1/2	11 3/4	3/4	12
10 1/4	1/2	12	3/4	12

Squares

Finished Size	Seam Allowance (inches)	Marked Size (inches)	Length in Yards (45" Width)	Number of Pieces
1"	1/4	1 1/2	1	667
2"	1/4	2 1/2	1	238
3"	1/4	3 1/2	1	120
3"	1/2	4	1	88
4"	1/4	4 1/2	1	63
4"	1/2	5	1	56
5"	1/2	6	7/8	35
6"	1/2	7	1	30
7"	1/2	8	1	20
8"	1/2	9	7/8	12
9"	1/2	10	7/8	12
10"	1/2	11	1	12
11"	1/2	12	3/4	6
12"	1/2	13	3/4	6

Quarter of a Square Triangles

(Divide by 2 for the Number of Combinations)

Finished Size	Seam Allowance	Marked Size	Length in Yards	Number of Pieces
3/4	1/4	2	1	1496
1	1/4	2 1/4	1	1140
1 3/4	1/4	3	1	616
2	1/4	3 1/4	1	520
2 3/4	1/4	4	1	352
3	1/4	4 1/4	1	320
3	1/2	5 1/2	1	192
3 1/2	1/2	6	7/8	140
4	1/2	6 1/2	1	120
4 1/2	1/2	7	1	120
5	1/2	7 1/2	7/8	80
5 1/2	1/2	8	1	80
6	1/2	8 1/2	1	80
6 1/2	1/2	9	7/8	48
7	1/2	9 1/2	7/8	48
7 1/2	1/2	10	7/8	48
8	1/2	10 1/2	1	48
8 1/2	1/2	11	1	48
9	1/2	11 1/2	3/4	24
9 1/2	1/2	12	3/4	24
10	1/2	12 1/2	3/4	24

Other Books of Special Interest to Quick Quiltmakers

CONTINUOUS CURVE QUILTING by Barbara Johannah, Pride of the Forest, $8.95, 8½" x 11", 56 pages.
A method of machine quilting pieced patterns which is adapted to the unique attributes of sewing machines. Continuous Curve Quilting is the sewing machine equivalent of hand quilting. You quilt in the area that you want to and then move easily to the next area to be quilted without finishing off and beginning new threads. You accomplish this by quilting in gentle arcs going through the corners to reach the next area to be quilted. This minimizes the number of starts and stops. Continuous Curve Quilting is ideal for those quilting patterns which have a figure/background relationship. It holds the layers together. It quilts the background areas only of your pattern giving your quilt a three dimensional effect. Available at Quilt Shops and from Pride of the Forest, RPO 7266, Menlo Park, CA 94025 for 8.95 plus $1.00 for shipping. California residents add $.54 sales tax.

MACHINE QUILTING by Robbie and Tony Fanning, Chilton, $9.95, 7" x 10", 334 pages. While Continuous Curve Quilting covers the 'where' of machine quilting, this book covers the 'how'. All its variations are covered in this comprehensive book. There is much to learn and this book accompanied by some practice will give you the answers. The most valuable sections for me are those on troubleshooting-specific answers on how to correct specific problems. It is a reference book to refer to over and over. A must buy if you are serious about machine quilting. Available at Quilt Shops and from Pride of the Forest, WPO 7266, Menlo Park, CA 94025 for $9.95. California residents add $.60 sales tax.

PRACTICAL MACHINE QUILTING FOR THE HOMEMAKER by Ernest B. Haight, self-published. $2.00 postpaid, 8½" x 11", 12 pages.
A wealth of practical ideas from one of the most logical thinkers in quiltmaking. Ernest gives his ideas on efficient piecing as well as his unique and simple method for quilting a rectangular quilt whole. It is, I think, especially suited to such quilts as Sunshine and Shadow and Trip Around the World. Available from Ernest B. Haight, RFD 1, David City, NE 68632.

QUICK QUILTING-Make a Quilt this Weekend by Barbara Johannah, Drake Publishers, Inc., $6.95, 8½" x 11", 144 pages.
The original book on making pieced patterns fast and efficiently. The primary focus of the book is on how to make patterns composed of squares, rectangles and half square triangles. No longer available.

THE QUILT PATTERN INDEX by Linda Shogren, Quilting Publications, $4.95 postpaid, 9" x 11", 49 pages.
If you have an extensive quilt book collection, Linda's index pulls it all together. If you are thinking of doing a log cabin, for example, but want to see some color combinations and setting arrangements first, look up log cabin. You will find a list of books and magazines in which it appears. It is so much easier than looking through each book and magazine one by one. Quilting Publications, 566 30th Avenue, San Mateo, California 94403.

As many of you know, it is traditional to have an intentional mistake in your quilt so as not to invite the wrath of God by creating a perfect thing. Books are not quite the same. There is seldom a need to make an intentional mistake because you can count on several unintentional ones slipping by you.

I have gone over the book and over it looking for those errors, but I am certain a few have slipped by me. If you find an error in yardage, number of pieces, etc. in the first year after the book is out, let me know in care of the Publisher. Thank you.

Happy Quilting,

Barbara Johannah

PRIDE OF THE FOREST
RPO 7266
Menlo Park, California 94025

Please send me _____ copies of THE QUICK QUILTMAKING HANDBOOK
@ $8.95 plus $1.00 shipping cost. California residents please add $.54 sales tax.

Enclosed is my check or money order for $_____.

Name _____

Address _____

_____ Zip _____